ORIENTAL RESPONSES
TO THE WEST

ORIENTAL RESPONSES TO THE WEST

COMPARATIVE ESSAYS IN SELECT WRITERS FROM THE MUSLIM WORLD

NASRIN RAHIMIEH

E.J. BRILL
LEIDEN • NEW YORK • KØBENHAVN • KÖLN
1990

ISBN 90 04 09177 7

© Copyright 1990 by E. J. Brill, Leiden, The Netherlands

All rights reserved. No part of this book may be reproduced or translated in any form, by print, photoprint, microfilm, microfiche or any other means without written permission from the publisher

PRINTED IN THE NETHERLANDS

For Askar and Xerxes Rahimieh

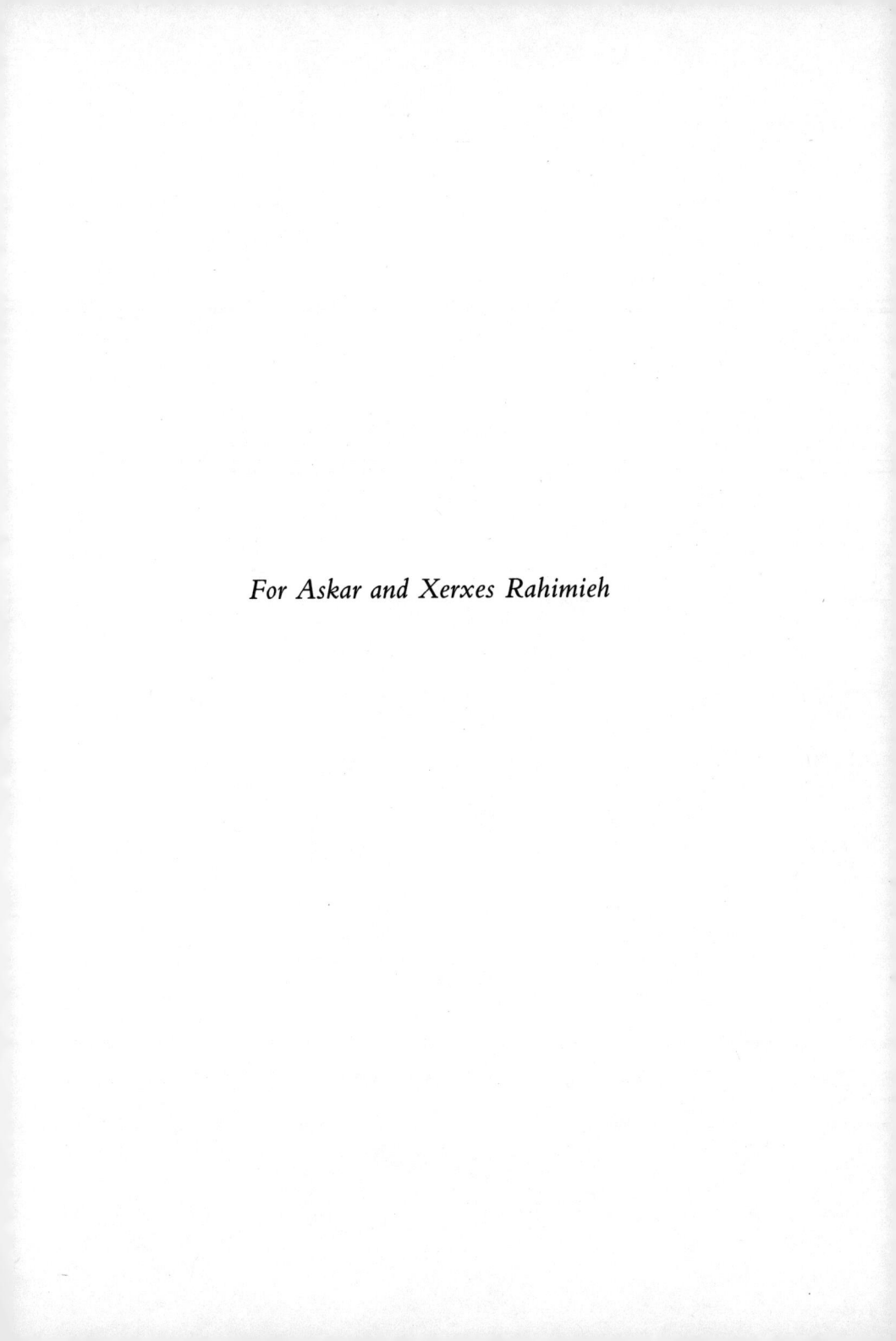

Contents

Preface ix

Introduction 1

   Chapter One

Descriptions of the West: Personal Encounters 13

   Chapter Two

A Double Dilemma: Oriental Women's Encounter with the West   37

   Chapter Three

The Voice of the Cross-Cultural Writer 55

   Chapter Four

Writing in the Step-Mother Tongue 72

   Chapter Five

Satirical Treatments of the East-West Encounter 89

   Chapter Six

Some "Neo-Islamic" Responses 100

Conclusion 111

Bibliography 118

Index 123

Preface

The ideas behind this book may be easily traceable to the renewed interest in the field of Orientalism. With my own roots in Iran, today one of the so-called trouble areas of the Middle East, I have been particularly drawn to the recent debates concerning Western approaches to the Islamic East. What has continuously struck me in these discussions is the sustained focus on the West. Even those who reject traditional views and stereotypes of the East hardly ever reach beyond the rhetoric of their rejection. The crucial and corresponding question regarding Eastern representations of the West is never asked. The point is not to find equivalents to the Western stereotypes, but rather to modulate the Eurocentrism which marks the exchanges between the Islamic East and the West. In a period of increased hostility between these two worlds, the time has come to better "Orient" ourselves and to open a dialogue, however discordant it may be. My study attempts to do so and, therefore, its focus is on cross-culturalism as perceived by writers and scholars from the Muslim world. Its descriptive nature is a function of my own experiences in crossing linguistic and national boundaries, and is intended to provoke further discussion and analysis.

In the years that have led to the completion of this book I have benefited from the help and encouragement of many individuals and institutions. In particular, I would like to express my gratitude to Milan V. Dimić of The University of Alberta for his relentless support and spirit of innovation, and Fouad Ajami of Johns Hopkins University for his careful reading of an earlier version. Special thanks are also due to my dear friend, Stan Beeler, who has helped in resolving technical problems and editing this book and, more importantly, has endured this project in many stages. Finally, I am indebted to The Social Sciences and Humanities Research Council of Canada and The Province of Alberta Heritage Fund for grants which made research and gathering of material possible.

Parts of some chapters of this book have appeared in articles in *World Literature Today*, *The Comparatist*, *The Canadian Review of Comparative Literature*, and a chapter of the book *Literature and Commitment* edited by Govind Narain Sharma.

Introduction

"The religion of Islam . . . hates and proscribes everything concrete; its God is the absolute One, in relation to whom human beings retain for themselves no purpose, no private domain, nothing peculiar to themselves."[1] So states Hegel in his *Lectures on the Philosophy of Religion*, a passage which is paradigmatic of much Western discourse on the Orient.

The opposition Hegel posits between the particular (the West) and the absolute (the East) allows for ever-changing patterns within Western thought, but relegates the Islamic East to its eternal and faithful single-minded abstractions. The apparent lack of individuality and originality which Hegel attributes to the Orient gives him licence not only to speak on its behalf, as if the distinct traditions of the Orient constitute a monolithic entity, but also to obliterate the authentic voices of the East from discussions of its customs, religions, and cultures. The Islamic Orient and its inhabitants become mere "objects" of someone else's thought.

The details and manners of the Western perception of the Orient have been documented, analyzed, and catalogued by generations of scholars. There is no need to restate or to summarize the general trends of these "reception" studies. Instead, what deserves attention is the conspicuous absence of an unmediated Orient from Western writing about the East. By absence I do not wish to imply the West was ignorant of all matters pertaining to Eastern literature and culture, but rather that "it" was reluctant to allow the different regions of the Orient to speak in their own voices. As Hegel's statement exemplifies, the focus is always on the West and *its* reactions to the East. Traditionally, there has been little attempt to compare and contrast Western perceptions of the Orient with Orientals' responses to the West. Despite the efforts of scholars like

---

[1] R. F. Brown et al., trans., Peter C. Hodgson, ed. (Berkeley: University of California Press, 1985) 243.

Raymond Schwab,[2] Norman Daniel,[3] and Kurt Goldhammer,[4] who have examined Western attitudes towards the East in a more critical light, the exchange has so far been rather one-sided.

Has the Orient remained silent while Western writers and scholars alike have discoursed upon its civilization and literature? At first, there does not appear to exist an equivalent system of representation of the West in the Oriental literary tradition. Edward Said, for one, points out: "To speak of scholarly specialization as a geographical 'field' is, in the case of Orientalism, fairly revealing since no one is likely to imagine a field symmetrical to it called Occidentalism."[5] Although one is inclined to agree with Said's statement, the question remains: what does the Orient have to offer as responses to the "Orientalist discourse?"[6]

My contention is that the Orient has never been and is not now a silent addressee. The absence of an Oriental voice in Western letters does not necessarily reflect total silence on the subject of the West in Oriental literature and criticism. Throughout the centuries of contact between the two cultures there have been treatises written by both sides on the general character and customs of the other. If, during the Crusades, the Christians stereotyped their enemy, their Muslim counterparts elaborated an equivalent myth, that of the ferocious Franks or *Rum*.

In a later phase of Islamic history, a traveller like Ibn Batoutah (fourteenth century A.D.) likewise adhered to the notion of the inherent superiority of the Muslim conquerors. During his visit to Gibraltar, for instance, he sees all improvements as a consequence of the Muslim presence:

> Cette place n'était pas alors dans l'état où elle se trouve maintenant . . . Cette partie qu'il [Aboû Haçan] a ajouté est la plus remarquable, et celle dont l'utilité est la plus générale. Il fit porter à Gibraltar d'abondantes munitions de guerre, ainsi que de bouche, et des provisions de toutes sortes; il agit en

---

[2] *La Renaissance orientale* (Paris: Payot, 1950).
[3] *Islam and the West: The Making of an Image* (Edinburgh: University Press, 1960).
[4] *Der Mythus von Ost und West: Eine Kultur-und religionsgeschichtliche Betrachtung* (München: Ernst Reinhardt, 1962).
[5] *Orientalism* (1978; rpt. New York: Vintage, 1979) 50.
[6] In his study of Orientalism, Edward Said has defined Orientalism as a "discourse," in Foucault's sense of the word: "a Western style for dominating, restructuring, and having authority over the Orient." (3)

cela envers l'Etre suprême avec la meilleure intention et la piété la plus sincère.[7]

Early Ottoman historians abandoned all pretence of objectivity in their accounts of encounters between East and West. The well-known chronicler, Ahmed Sinân Celebi, uses one term to refer to all European nations, the "infidel," and seizes every opportunity to expatiate upon the moral flaws of the Europeans. In the following statement, he revels over the possibility of a Christian monarch's illegitimate birth:

> Zu dieser Zeit, im Jahre 897 [1491] kam die frohe Kunde, daß des König Mathias geizige Seele zugrunde gegangen und sein unreiner Körper in die Hölle gefahren ist—wodurch sich die Hilfe und Gnade Allâhs in besonderer Weise gezeigt hat—und seine Dynastie, die von schlechtem Ursprung war, dadurch ausgestorben ist; und man sagte, daß diese Dynastie, gleich einem Esel ist, dem der Schwanz abgeschnitten wurde, zugrunde ging ... Er hinterließ einen Sohn namens Imre [Johannes Corvinus], der von einer Dirne stammt.[8]

Such systematic emphasis on the distinctions between the self and the other is very reminiscent of the European portrayals of Orientals. What both Rana Kabbani[9] and Edward Said[10] see as unique features of the European approach to the Orient and the Orientals may well be instead a universal of cultural encounter. The imposition of distance and difference both in early Muslim chronicles and European writing about the Islamic East is characteristic of descriptions of the unknown. In providing the

---

[7] C. Defrémery and B. R. Sanguinetti, *Voyages d'Ibn Batoutah, texte arabe accompagné d'une traduction*, Vol. IV (Paris: Imprimerie Nationale, 1879) 356.

[8] Brigitte Moser, trans. and ed., *Die Chronik des Ahmed Sinân Celebi genannt Bihisti: Eine Quelle zur Geschichte des Osmanischen Reiches unter Sultan Bâyezid II*, Beiträge zur Kenntnis Südeuropas und des nahen Orients (München: Dr. Dr. Rudolf Trofenik, 1980) 134.

[9] "In the European narration of the Orient, there was a deliberate stress on those qualities that made the East different from the West, exiled it into an irretrievable 'otherness.'" Rana Kabbani, *Europe's Myths of Orient* (Bloomington: Indiana University Press, 1986) 5–6.

[10] "I shall be calling *Orientalism*, a way of coming to terms with the Orient that is based on the Orient's special place in European Western experience. The Orient is not only adjacent to Europe: it is also the place of Europe's greatest and richest and oldest colonies, the source of its civilizations and languages, its cultural contestant, and one of its deepest and most recurring images of the Other." (1)

readers with "objective" views of an alien society, the observer has to rely on either the familiar or the alien. The path to the culture, language, or civilization of the other is frequently through comparisons and contrasts, figures which are inherently polar.

During his visits to France, the nineteenth-century Persian monarch, Nasir ud-Din Shah, adopts such a comparative approach towards the French and their civilization. The Shah is careful to draw parallels between France and his own country. The reader is introduced at once to an exotic and to a familiar setting: "Paris is a beautiful and graceful city, with a delicious climate. It generally enjoys sunshine, thus much resembling the climate of Persia."[11] Given that the King's diaries were at the time the only account of France accessible to Iranians, observations like the following, in the mind of his audience, became more than passing: "the cities of Firangistan (Europe in general) all resemble one another. When one has been seen, the arrangement, condition, and scale of the others is in one's possession" (105). Nasir ud-Din Shah's approach to the unfamiliar culture of the French is not essentially different from the ways in which Europeans recorded their encounters with Orientals. If there is a difference, it is in the assumption of superiority on the part of the West which in the heyday of colonialism became central to the self-image of the Westerner in the East.

For historical reasons there is no need to elaborate upon, it became increasingly difficult for the East to escape its systematic reduction to a handful of traits, and the Oriental's image of himself was tainted with Western impressions of him. That figures of authority in the East also took to imitation of Western manners reinforced this assimilation of the other's viewpoint. For example, the Persian Kings returned from their European journeys determined to "westernize" their country and to adopt European customs and dress codes. As reflected in the title of the following poem by Mohammad Iqbal, in the course of their encounters the Eastern observers became "Dazzled by Europe":

> Your light is only Europe's light reflected:
> You are four walls her architects have built;

---

[11] J. W. Redhouse, trans., *The Diary of H. M. The Shah of Persia* (London: John Murray, 1874) 224.

> A shell of dry mud with no tenant soul,
> An empty scabbard chased with flowery gilt.
>
> To your mind God's existence seems unproved:
> Your own existence not proved to mine.
> He whose life shines like a gem, alone exists;
> Take heed to it! I do not see yours shine.[12]

In the modern era, this enthusiasm for a Western lifestyle has sometimes been translated into a passive acceptance of all that is imported from the West. Western influence in the East has gone beyond importation of technological advances and material goods, and, as a result, the West has left an indelible impression of its own superiority on the intellectual life of the East.

In *Orientalism* as in his later works, Edward Said laments the too easy acceptance by the East of the image carved for it by the West: ". . . if all told there is an intellectual acquiescence in the images and doctrines of Orientalism, there is also a very powerful reinforcement of this in economic, political, and social exchange: the modern Orient, in short, participates in its own Orientalizing" (325). The note of despair in Said's statement is also a protest giving rise to hope. Are not Said's despair and self-reproach, in fact, attempts to break away from the tradition of Oriental acceptance of Western stereotypes? When, in *After the Last Sky*, Said tries to come to terms, as a Palestinian, with life in exile, he is effectively shattering the silence of the East. Aware of the difficulties in challenging dominant Western beliefs, he nevertheless seeks means of asserting himself:

> What I have been saying is that we ourselves provide not enough of a presence to force the untidiness of life into a coherent pattern of our own making. At best, to judge simply from my case, we can read ourselves against another people's pattern, but since it is not ours—even though we are its designated enemy—we emerge as its effects, its errata, its counter-narratives. Whenever we try to narrate ourselves, we appear as dislocations in *their* discourse.[13]

---

[12] V. G. Kiernan, trans., in *Modern Islamic Literature from 1800 to the Present*, James Kritzeck, ed. (New York: Mentor, 1970) 82.
[13] Edward W. Said, *After the Last Sky: Palestinian Lives* Photographs by Jean Mohr (New York: Pantheon, 1986) 140.

Said is not alone in his questioning of the Western stereotypical images of the East and in his reproach of Orientals who reinforce these stereotypes. In recent years, many scholars of Eastern origin have undertaken re-examinations of Western representations of the Orient: Rana Kabbani, Abdelkebir Khatibi and Asaf Hussain, to name a few. What is interesting about the body of work produced by these scholars is its shift from the Western perspective, i.e. the dominant and almost canonical, to a more critical outlook which rejects the categorical exclusion of the East from discussions of its literature and culture. The aim of this group of scholars, who for the most part are immersed in both cultures, is, as Khatibi points out, to dislodge the domination of the Western norms which have gained unchallenged authority in the East as well as the West:

> . . . nous voulons décentrer en nous le savoir occidental, nous décentrer par rapport à ce centre, à cette origine que se donne l'Occident. Cela en opérant déjà dans le champ d'une pensée plurielle et planétaire, différence qui s'acharne contre sa réduction et sa domestication.[14]

Khatibi addresses not only the Occident, but also the self-image of the Oriental. This viewpoint is crucial to any "new approach" to the study of East-West relations. Orientalism cannot and must not be replaced with a new discipline, Occidentalism, which would constitute a mere displacement of xenophobia. Like Khatibi, Said sets the elimination of cultural barriers as his primary objective:

> If [*Orientalism*] stimulates a new kind of dealing with the Orient, indeed if it eliminates the "Orient" and "Occident" altogether, then we shall have advanced a little in the process of what Raymond Williams has called the "unlearning" of "the inherent dominative mode." (28)

The conditional "if" in Said's statement is indicative of the problematic nature of the task before these scholars. Their first step is to recover the Orient from the centuries of imposed silence in the realm of criticism and methodology. Hence Said's interest in the theoretical aspects of the study of Orientalism. He defines Orientalism as a form of discourse within the larger context of Foucault's theories of knowledge and power. Khatibi, in his study of post-colonialism in North Africa, relies heavily upon

---

[14] Abdelkebir Khatibi, *Maghreb pluriel* (Paris: Denoël, 1983) 54.

Derrida's theories. This is not to say that all criticisms of Orientalism have originated from scholars immersed in European education and life. Many writers and critics residing in the East had already paved the way for the most recent trends in the study of the Orient.

In this day and age, however, one cannot speak of Orientalism without acknowledging and situating Edward Said's pioneering work. It is he who is responsible for the currency of "Orientalism" and the tone of a new polemic deeply rooted in personal experience.

In the introduction to *Orientalism*, Said expresses his motives, which have since become the cornerstone of anti-Orientalist treatises, in the following manner:

> Much of the personal investment in this study derives from my awareness of being an "Oriental" as a child growing up in two British colonies. All of my education, in those colonies (Palestine and Egypt) and in the United States, has been Western, and yet that deep early awareness has persisted. In many ways my study of Orientalism has been an attempt to inventory the traces upon me, the Oriental subject, of the culture whose domination has been so powerful a factor in the life of all Orientals. (25)

To argue effectively, Said has had to adopt a dual vision and play the part of both subject and subjugator. A telling reminder of the tension which lies beneath his rhetoric of duality is a passage in *After the Last Sky*. In spite of his personal identification with the issues of Palestinian exile, in writing about them he finds himself resorting to the perspective of both the insider and the outsider:

> This is not an objective book. Our intention was to show Palestinians through Palestinian eyes without minimizing the extent to which even to themselves they feel different, or "other" . . . We also felt that [the photographer, Jean Mohr] saw us as we would have seen ourselves—at once inside and outside our world. The same double vision informs my text. As I wrote, I found myself switching pronouns, from "we" to "you" to "they," to designate Palestinians. As abrupt as these shifts are, I feel they reproduce the way "we" experience ourselves, the way "you" sense that others look at you, the way, in your solitude, you feel the distance between "you" and where "they" are. (6)

Written in the language of the "other" and primarily directed towards a Western audience, Said's treatises, nevertheless, have a secondary internal focus; in rejecting the Western stereotypes of the Orient and calling for a better understanding of the modern Orient, he demands a more active participation of Eastern societies in the study of their own cultures. Although *Orientalism* cannot be singled out as the first critical survey of the Western attitudes towards the East, when it was published, in 1978, it was the first scholarly articulation of the same *Zeitgeist* which produced historical events such as the 1979 revolution in Iran. I am not suggesting that the Iranian revolution be understood purely in terms of Said's speculations, but rather that both the book and the event be regarded as Oriental responses to the West.

Said attributes to Orientalism three interdependent designations: 1) Orientalism as an academic discipline, 2) Orientalism "as a style of thought based on an ontological and epistemological distinction made between 'the Orient' and (most often) 'the Occident'" (2), and 3) Orientalism as a Foucaltian discourse, otherwise defined as "a Western style for dominating, restructuring, and having authority over the Orient" (3). It is this third definition which forms the methodological basis of Said's study; ultimately, Orientalism is to be seen as an "archival system"[15] in all of its spheres of endeavour—political, academic, and artistic. Following this argument, Said suggests that no Westerner who came into contact with the East or wrote about it was, or is, able to escape the discursive consistency of his predecessors. In the realm of literature this means that texts as different as Goethe's *West-Östlicher Divan*, Nerval's *Voyage en Orient*, and T. E. Lawrence's *Seven Pillars of Wisdom* are variants of the same thematic treatment of the Orient. Orientals are represented as Europe's "surrogate" or "underground self" (3), that is to say, as dependent upon the West.

Secondly, Said argues that this timeless image of the Orient was deliberately reinforced by Western colonial powers. In this sense, the enterprise of even the academic Orientalist was inextricably linked with the political ambitions of Western hegemonies. In Massignon's seemingly sympathetic rhetoric, for example, Said finds the linguistic apparatus of an empire:

> . . . the Oriental, *en soi*, was incapable of appreciating or understanding

[15] As defined in Michel Foucault's *L'Archéologie du savoir* (Paris: Gallimard, 1969).

himself. Partly because of what Europe had done to him, he had lost his religion and his *philosophie*; Muslims had "un vide immense" within them; they were close to anarchy and suicide. It became France's obligation, then, to associate itself with the Muslims' desire to defend their traditional culture, the rule of their dynastic life, and the patrimony of believers. (271)

In the modern phase of Orientalism, especially as practiced in the American institutions, Said detects a waning of this pretence of interest in the preservation of Muslim identity. Instead, modern Orientalists reduce Orientals to abstractions such as "attitudes" and "trends," further denying them an independent culture and identity (291).

Although Said's thesis is well-grounded in historical evidence, it suffers from certain methodological weaknesses which threaten to undermine the validity of the overall argument. If one accepts the premise that all representations of the Islamic East, by virtue of being embedded in the archives of knowledge of the European representers, are misrepresentations, one wonders how it is possible to break through the discursive consistency which encompasses all cross-cultural contacts. To overcome this dilemma, Said wavers between two incompatible positions. He adopts Foucault's definitions and insists that all representations are dictated by collective cultural preconceptions;[16] but also attempts to allow for marks of individuality: ". . . unlike Michel Foucault, to whose work I am greatly indebted, I do believe in the determining imprint of individual writers upon the otherwise anonymous collective body of texts constituting a discursive formation like Orientalism" (23). In practice, though, aside from certain historically-determined nuances, Said finds little difference in the works of European Orientalists from the Middle Ages to modernity. His own analysis reveals that the struggle between individuality and discursive formation results in the confirmation of anonymity.

A second conclusion to be drawn from Said's thesis, one hardly ever

---

[16] "The real issue is whether indeed there can be a true representation of anything, or whether any and all representations, because they *are* representations, are embedded first in the language and then in the culture, institutions, and political ambience of the representer. If the latter alternative is the correct one (as I believe it is), then we must be prepared to accept the fact that a representation is *eo ipso* implicated, intertwined, embedded, interwoven with a great many other things besides the 'truth,' which is itself a representation." (272)

discussed by Said and his followers, is the impossibility of unbiased Eastern representations of the West, for the East is also subject to a set of cultural, ideological, and religious prejudices. The question which haunts Said's study is whether representations of other cultures can be redefined in a manner that would lead to the "[elimination of] 'Orient' and 'Occident' altogether" (28).

In *Covering Islam: How the Media and the Experts Determine How We See the Rest of the World*, Said addresses some of the problematic and pragmatic issues which emerge from *Orientalism*. Part of this second study deals with the Islamic world's responses to the West. In the American media's coverage of Islam, he rediscovers the persistence of the "Orientalist discourse." Examples such as the American coverage of the hostage dilemma in Iran or the public execution of a Saudi princess confirm that the media merely reiterate what is dictated by a tradition of distortion and manipulation:

> . . . covering Islam is not interpretation in the genuine sense but an assertion of power. The media say what they wish about Islam because they can, with the result that Islamic punishment and "good" Muslims (in Afghanistan, for instance) dominate the scene indiscriminately; little else is covered because anything falling outside the consensus definition of what is important is considered irrelevant to the United States interests and to the media's definition of a good story.[17]

Reciprocally, the Muslim East responds in exaggerated gestures, which further reinforce an already faulty Western perception. Direct encounter is, therefore, reduced to further instances of rhetorical exchange:

> Muslim self-identity has . . . tended to be strengthened by losing encounters with a monolithic block representing itself as "Western civilization," and sensing this, the West's own demagogues inveigh against medieval fanaticism and cruel tyranny. For almost every Muslim, the mere assertion of an Islamic identity becomes an act of nearly cosmic defiance and a necessity for survival. War seems an extremely logical outcome. (72)

Said's analysis implies that for Muslims, as well, there exists little possibility of breaking away from the dominant discourse. The best example of this double distortion is, to return to one of Said's own

---

[17] Edward Said, *Covering Islam* (New York: Pantheon, 1981) 142.

examples, the hostage episode in Iran. It was clear, that in the course of what they believed to be a calculated manipulation of the American media and public opinion, the hostage holders themselves became victims of the camera and their own rhetoric. As a result, both sides failed to cross the barriers separating them and fell back upon the stereotypes of the other.

Although, in *Covering Islam*, Said presents a more balanced description of the communication deadlock between the Muslim world and the West, he is still reluctant to realize fully the consequences of his own theoretical premise. That is, the Islamic world's understanding and treatment of the West are not exempt from the type of biases Said attributes to the discipline of Orientalism.

Without wishing to inaugurate a new field of study under the title of "Occidentalism," I would like to suggest that there exists in modern Oriental fiction and criticism a class of writing whose primary thematic and ideological preoccupation is the Western treatment of the Orient and its reflection in the psyche of Eastern intellectuals. My understanding of the term "Oriental" in this context is not limited to the writer's linguistic preferences; as intimated from the examples mentioned thus far, it is not unusual for critics and writers of Oriental parentage to choose to write in a European language. In fact, the cases in which a deliberate choice is made against one's native language so as to reach a wider audience bring much more complex cross-cultural issues into play.

My aim is not to reduce the large body of Eastern writing about the West to neatly-compartmentalized units for academic reference, but rather to examine the area of East-West literary and cultural relations in a broader light and from a less Eurocentric viewpoint.

A study of this scope and nature must be subject to certain limitations. In order to expand the focus of my study, I have selected texts of the modern period from a number of Eastern countries by writers using languages ranging from Arabic, to Persian, Turkish, English, French, and German. In spite of steps taken to present a fair sample of Eastern writing about the West, I realize that my own linguistic limitations or unavailability of works in North American libraries creates gaps in the corpus. I wish to stress that my work does not claim to be an exhaustive treatment of the subject matter. I only hope to provide a general framework for approaching literary and critical works by authors from the Islamic East who have directly or indirectly confronted the West in its treatment of their own cultures and societies. In particular, it should be noted that I am not addressing the traditional fields of Arabic, Persian, Turkish, and Indian literatures, rather works which like their authors straddle worlds and conventions of any given discipline. Following the same spirit, I have, when possible, quoted from European-language translations of texts. Unless otherwise noted English translations are my own.

I have also deliberately resisted the temptation to apply labels to groups of texts, because I see my field of study as dynamic and constantly shifting. To fix the reactions of certain authors in rigidly-defined categories would de-emphasize the dynamic nature of the phenomena I will be describing. Related to this is another decision I came to early in my work, that the more abstruse terms and approaches of some contemporary critics would be of little use to either myself or my readers. Thus, while the subject matter of *Oriental Responses to the West* is very untraditional, my methodology and my critical apparatus are quite traditional.

That the Islamic Orient has finally "taken heed" of Iqbal's criticism and has risen to meet the challenge of the West is evident. It may be possible to say that Orientals are no longer "dazzled by Europe," but they are still plagued by a history of misunderstandings and misrepresentations. It is the ways in which the East has begun to come to terms with these issues, crucial to its self-definition, that must be analyzed in a comprehensive fashion if there is to exist any understanding between East and West.

Chapter One
Descriptions of the West: Personal Encounters

> Let me . . . confess before the Divine majesty of God, how content I am to be a Christian, and I have at last lost all memory of natural pain I once felt at finding myself cut off for ever from my wife, my son, my country and all I there possessed.[1]
>
> (Uruch Beg)

This statement by Uruch Beg, a seventeenth-century Persian emissary who converted to Catholicism in Europe, not only demonstrates its author's precarious position between two cultures, but also belies Bernard Lewis's assumption that "during the early formative centuries, Muslims displayed an extraordinary reluctance, grounded in law as well as tradition, to travel in Christian Europe."[2] Many Muslims did indeed travel in the West. Moreover, like their European counterparts, their reception of Western mores and thought was multifaceted and complex.

Although my intention is not to provide a historical survey of the instances of travel in the West, I have found it useful to trace some of the early prototypes of the personal encounters which exerted an influence on the literature of the modern era. Uruch Beg's narration of his travels in Europe is one such.

Uruch Beg left Iran in 1599 as one of the four secretaries to the Persian ambassador whom Shah Abbas had sent to the princes of Europe under the guidance of Sir Anthony Sherley. In 1602, shortly before the ambassador was to have returned to Iran, three of his secretaries, including Uruch Beg, embraced the Catholic faith and abandoned their official

---

[1] G. Le Strange, trans. and ed. *Don Juan of Persia: A Shi'ah Catholic*, The Broadway Travellers Series (London: George Routledge, 1926) 308.
[2] Bernard Lewis, *The Muslim Discovery of Europe* (New York: W. W. Norton, 1982) 91.

post. Although the circumstances leading to the conversion are not fully explained, the date of the mission suggests a conflict between the secretaries' own beliefs and Shi'ism, at that time the newly-declared state religion in Iran. Uruch Beg's own explanation, clearly intended as a declaration of faith, offers very little insight into the reasons for his sudden conversion:

> . . . as soon as I had got to Valladolid I went to see Ali Quli Beg at the Jesuit House, and no sooner had I begun to talk with him, and to hold converse with the Fathers of the Society of Jesus—religious men as discrete as they are learned—when it became manifest how God Almighty willed that a miracle should be worked in me. For I began immediately to feel an inordinate longing in my heart to seek and find His Divine Grace . . . as I was returned to my lodging house I urgently called upon the Fathers to grant me baptism, though no master had yet given me any sufficient instruction in religion. (299)

Despite its meticulous recording of events, the work, as a whole, provides only cursory glimpses of the author's personal impressions of Europe. Books One and Two are devoted to a survey of Iranian history and are believed to have been inserted by the editor, Remón. Book Three consists of Uruch Beg's own narrative. Even in this section, he offers a purely descriptive account of his experiences in Europe. However, no longer fearing retaliation, he is less reluctant to criticize the customs of his homeland. For instance, he speaks of Persian poetry with obvious disdain: "The Persians pride themselves much on their poets, and these, though without art, compose an infinity of verses" (54).[3] Yet it is clear that he still relishes his own traditions. The two chapters in which he relates daily life in Iran are composed in a less monotonous tone and offer more commentary. The contrasts between descriptions of Iran and Europe suggest that uncertainty about his fate in Europe dictated the manner of his presentation. In the final pages, as seen in the passage I have quoted in the opening of this chapter, he is unable to conceal his longing for his homeland and even his expression of gratitude becomes a means to confessing exile.

---

[3] It should be borne in mind that such remarks may have been the work of the Spanish editor.

The confessional note on which Uruch Beg's narrative ends is lacking throughout the diary of Nasir ud-Din Shah, the first Persian monarch to travel to Europe (in the 1870s). Refraining from criticism and evaluation of European customs, the Persian king sets out to recreate in painstaking detail his official meetings and excursions. In all of his descriptions Nasir ud-Din Shah maintains a distantly admiring perspective. Aside from the few aforementioned comparisons between European countries and Iran, in matters such as climate and food, the monarch does not draw specific conclusions from his observations. For the Shah, Europe constitutes a unified mass, despite differences in language and culture. He prefers to attribute general traits to the peoples of Europe, notwithstanding his own observations to the contrary. Although Nasir ud-Din Shah does not openly criticize any aspects of European life, his generalizations can be seen as covert commentary. In this sense, he is similar to some of his European counterparts who chose to reiterate commonplace images of the Orient, rather than elaborate on their own experiences: "Most travellers of the seventeenth century added practical observations of their own, but based their accounts of Islam as a religion, not on their own direct experience, but on tradition inherited from the medieval West" (Daniel 282). The main distinction between Nasir-ud Din Shah's accounts of European life and those of European travellers in the East is that in the case of the former there was no venerable tradition upon which the Persian monarch could rely. That is not to say, however, that the diary of the king is devoid of stereotypes. The account of the Shah's meeting with one of the Rothschild brothers in France is a case in point:

> [Rothschild] greatly advocated the cause of the Jews, mentioned the Jews of Persia, and claimed tranquility for them. I said to him: "I have heard that you, brothers, possess a thousand crores of money. I consider the best thing to do would be that you should pay fifty crores to some large or small state, and buy a territory in which you could collect all the Jews of the whole world, you becoming their chiefs, and leading them on their way in peace, so that you should no longer be thus scattered and dispersed." We laughed heartily, and he made no reply. (236–37)

Both Uruch Beg and Nasir-ud Din Shah observe Europe with curiosity and admiration, without revealing themselves as zealous advocates of westernization. Their attention to detail indicates that they saw themselves as intermediaries between Europe and Iran. There is, however, a clear distinction between Nasir ud-Din Shah's approach and that of Uruch Beg in their accounts of life in Europe. The Shah, aware of writing primarily for an Iranian audience, is more eager to comment upon European mores, while the Iranian convert, addressing himself to European audiences, devotes the greater part of his narrative to descriptions of his own country.

Uruch Beg's preoccupation with his heritage is shared by other Eastern travellers and emissaries who wrote in European languages. In *Three Centuries: Family Chronicles of Turkey and Egypt*, Emine Foat Tugay is less interested in presenting her impressions of Europe than in supplementing the Europeans' knowledge of "family life in the Ottoman Empire among the upper classes during the nineteenth and the beginning of the twentieth centuries."[4] The only chapter in which she speaks of her life in Europe, "Five Years Abroad," reduces that experience to a disappointing first encounter with French cuisine.

> I had never tasted foreign food and was looking forward to meals excitingly different from anything which I had known previously. My parents had engaged a French chef . . . [The preliminary courses] seemed disappointing to me, but then came the turkey . . . The first helping showed that something was lacking. Why was it stuffed with chestnuts, and where was the rice, the 'iç pilav,' flavoured with raisins, white pistachios, and the liver of the bird? I was told that this was the French way of serving turkey and that, abroad, rice is not eaten with it. It was too much . . . I burst into tears and had to leave the room. (242–43)

Entertaining as they may be, these self-portraits primarily destined for a European audience should be distinguished from travelogues and diaries of Eastern travellers who undertook detailed descriptions of manners and customs of Europeans.

In the later periods of contact, especially during the nineteenth century, personal accounts and translations provided the East with detailed information on the West. According to Ibrahim Abu-Lughod the Arab reader:

---

[4] Emine Foat Tugay, *Three Centuries: Family Chronicles of Turkey and Egypt* (London: Oxford University Press, 1963) author's note.

... would have had available to him a concrete image of the political, economic and natural geography of the world. The location and characteristics of European countries and, indeed, the remainder of the world in so far as it was known to European scholars, was made a part of his own *Weltanschauung*.[5]

One of the first Egyptian travellers to France in the nineteenth century, Rifa'a at-Tahtāwi composed a comprehensive account of French society, law, and customs for his compatriots in his *Description of Paris*.[6] In his official role as an imam accompanying an Egyptian educational mission to Paris, Tahtāwi perceived a need for familiarizing his country with the manners of the French. His goal was to bridge the gap between his own society and that of France. Tahtāwi attributed the differences between Europe and the Muslim world to the more advanced Western educational system: "Every man, whether rich or poor, has a book-case, as all the lower classes read and write."[7] Confronted with the superiority of the French in the educational sciences, Tahtāwi's only recourse was to bring about changes in his native land. After his return from Europe, he became director of the School of Languages in Cairo which was patterned after the school of Oriental Languages in Paris. As the director of this school, Tahtāwi supervised translations of technical, scientific, and literary works into Arabic.

Despite his enthusiasm for the French educational model, Tahtāwi was extremely selective in his choice of elements of French culture to be recommended for adoption by Egyptians. An interesting example of Tahtāwi's selectivity is his discussion of the role of women in French society. He is astounded by the European women's ability to compete with men in education and learning. Although later Tahtāwi himself encouraged the education of women in Egypt, he never ceased to regard European women as morally inferior to Muslim women: "They are like men in all that they do. You may even find among them young women who have an affair with a stranger without being married."[8]

[5] Ibrahim Abu-Lughod, *Arab Rediscovery of Europe: A Study in Cultural Encounters*, Oriental Studies 22 (Princeton: University Press, 1963) 54–5.

[6] The original title is *Takhlīs al-ibrīz fī takhlīs Parīz* (1834).

[7] Quoted in John A. Haywood's *Modern Arabic Literature 1800–1970: An Introduction with Extracts in Translation* (New York: St. Martin's, 1972) 75.

[8] Qtd. in Haywood 76.

In his encounter with the West, Tahtāwi would appear to have maintained a keen interest in the preservation of his own culture, or at least his own morality. Other Egyptians who followed Tahtāwi's example and travelled to Europe became even more obsessed with their national identity. In an attempt to overcome the sense of inferiority that the advancements in Europe produced in them, some looked back nostalgically to a prouder, though distant, past:

> Au départ, une forte prise de conscience, un sentiment d'infériorité vis-à-vis de l'Europe puissante et, en revanche, la conviction d'avoir eu le premier rang dans l'histoire. Cette phrase d'Ahmed le Fellah à Edmond About: 'Nos pères [. . .] ont créé de toutes pièces une civilisation parfaite quand tout était solitude ou barbarie dans vos pays,' résume bien des pages dictées par le voyage à Rifa'a à ses successeurs.[9]

This type of comparison was intended to discourage Easterners from total assimilation in the West. As contacts between East and West became more extensive, there were more signs of "anxiety of influence" among Eastern intellectuals. In 1869 the Lebanese writer, Butrus al-Bustāni, who himself had travelled in the West, warned the youth of his time against indiscriminate adoption of Western standards, or *tafarnuj* (westernization).[10]

Among the Arabs who visited Europe in the nineteenth century there were, nevertheless, those who idealized life in Europe. The exiled Egyptian journalist, Adīb Ishāq, painted an exaggerated image of French society which is clearly intended to emphasize the contrasts between France and Egypt. However, like Uruch Beg, Ishāq fails to disguise his personal suffering in exile:

> Sous un ciel d'équité, sur une terre paisible, parmi des hommes libres, là où se font entendre les concerts harmonieux d'une société fondée sur la justice, les gémissements que pousse mon peuple opprimé, sous les fouets des bourreaux, me viennent à la mémoire et je me prends à sangloter comme une mère venant de perdre son enfant.[11]

---

[9] Anouar Louca, *Voyageurs et écrivains égyptiens en France au XIXe Siècle* (Paris: Didier, 1970) 116.
[10] *Tafarnuj* literally means frankification.
[11] Qtd. in Louca 128.

The variety of contacts between East and West during the nineteenth century furnished the East with a better grasp of the West. The numerous descriptions of the West not only performed the function of introducing Western societies to the East, but also became a touchstone against which the East could measure itself. Some of the Indians who had witnessed the differences between England and India, for instance, held their own culture responsible for the lack of advancement:

> Indian poverty depressed many. A Hindu subassistant surgeon remarked sadly that Indians only copied the faults of the British. He did not think Indians would advance themselves "merely by wearing trousers and hats and smoking cigarettes and drinking wine." It was only by initiative, hard work and education that Indians could make progress, he thought.[12]

In its attempt to understand Europe, modern Orient also came to understand itself. Isa Sadiq, an Iranian student who was sent to England in the beginning of the twentieth century and was to become one of the leading figures responsible for reforms in the Iranian educational system, makes explicit the way in which travel and education in the West raised self-awareness in the Oriental observer:

> ... I also grasped something of the importance and depth of Persian culture ... After studying Persian literature and history for a year my love of country was based on strong foundations for I now realised that my country had played a major part in the civilisation of the world, and had nourished very great men in its bosom. It had given great literature and great art to the world.[13]

Even those who did not favour the adoption of Western customs were perforce drawn into the current which was to change the Orient's perception of itself. It is futile to perceive these reactions as effects of either westernization or influence; the range of Eastern responses to the West, even in the early days of contact between the two cultures, is far too varied and complex to warrant simplistic codification.

The argument against attributing these reactions to direct influence

---

[12] Rozina Visram, *Ayahs, Lascars and Princes: Indians in Britain 1700–1947* (London: Pluto, 1986) 136.
[13] Quoted by Denis Wright in *The Persians Amongst the English: Episodes in Anglo-Persian History* (London: I. B. Tauris, 1985) 150.

from the West is convincingly demonstrated by the actual complexity of literary exchange, which has by no means meant a block transfer of "Western ideas" into Eastern writing. Through their readings and translations of European sources, nineteenth-century Arab commentators and writers were able to experiment with literary forms which existed in their tradition but would not have otherwise flourished. Some Arab critics have regarded the use of translations as detrimental to the development of indigenous talent. Yet others like Mikha'il Nu'ayma deem translation to be a mode of literary exchange crucial to development:

> Let us translate. The beggar begs when he cannot support himself by the work of his own hands. The thirsty man begs his neighbor for water when his well dries up. We are poor, though we brag about our abundant wealth. Why, then, should we not attempt to satisfy our needs from the abundance of others which is available to us? We are in a stage of literary and social development in which we have become aware of many intellectual needs. These needs were never known to us before our recent contact with the West. We have no sufficient number of pens or brains to satisfy these intellectual needs. Therefore, let us translate.[14]

Mikha'il Nu'ayma's assertions find support in episodes from the literary history of Egypt. As pointed out by Anouar Louca, the development of modern Egyptian prose forms such as the essay and the novel can be traced to the age of travel: ". . . c'est à deux genres différents que la relation de voyage donne naissance: l'essai et le roman. L'essai n'est pas une nouveauté pour la littérature arabe. Mais dans des styles plus variés, il expose maintenant des réflexions sociales, politiques et culturelles d'une portée moderne" (241).[15]

An even more interesting example of the type of literary fusion made possible though such contacts is the reception and adoption of the

---

[14] Quoted by Matti Moosa in *The Origins of Modern Arabic Fiction* (Washington, D.C.: Three Continents, 1983) 68–9.

[15] As further evidence in support of this point, Abu-Lughod points out: "The impact on Arab methodology is even clearer. A brief comparison between the late nineteenth- and early twentieth century literature and that of the preceding period clearly reveals some basic changes. The earlier works appear to the Western reader to be capriciously ordered collections of heterogeneous thoughts. In contrast, the later works are comparatively well organized in their presentation. (63–4)

Englishman James Morier's novel, *The Adventures of Hajji Baba of Isphahan* (1824), in the history of Persian literature.

In the frame story of this novel, the fictional Persian narrator speaks apologetically of his compatriots' inherent disinclination towards objective and analytical observation of foreigners:

> Ever since I have known your nation [the British], I have remarked their inquisitiveness, and eagerness after knowledge. Whenever I have travelled with them, I observed they record their observations in books; and when they return home, thus make their fellow countrymen acquainted with the most distant regions of the globe. Will you believe me, that I, Persian, as I am, have followed their example, hence, during the period of my residence at Constantinople, I have passed my time in writing a detailed history of my life . . . I think it would not fail to create an interest if published in Europe?[16]

As a representative of his nation, Hajji Baba is shown to be certain that his personal diary would be appreciated in Europe and not in his native land. This characterization of Iranians corresponds to other Western stereotypes of the East; what Orientals learn by way of imitation from the West remains, by and large, beyond their comprehension.

The impulse to relegate Morier's fictional account of the Persian character, "Persian as I am," to the ranks of Orientalist writing is, however, to be mitigated by the irony of the fact that "many Iranians do not realize that *Hajji Baba* is the creation of a foreigner."[17] The 1905 Persian translation of Morier's book became popular in Iran, albeit in the small circle of the educated elite, and contributed to the development of modern Persian prose.[18]

The enthusiastic reception of the Persian translation of Morier's novel and the seemingly passive acceptance of its stereotypes of Persians by the

---

[16] James Morier, *The Adventures of Hajji Baba of Isphahan* (New York: Random House, 1937), first published in 1824, no pagination is provided for the frame story in this edition.

[17] William O. Beeman, *Language, Status, and Power in Iran* (Bloomington: Indiana University Press, 1986) 238.

[18] "In 1905 the Persian text of *Hajji Baba* was published in Calcutta, after the English version by James Morier. The Persian edition set a standard for modern writing in the language of the people. The vernacular is reproduced with all the grace and liveliness of ordinary Persian speech. This book is one of the most important memorials in the new style of Persian prose." Peter Avery, "Developments in Modern Persian Prose, (1920s–1950s)" in *Critical Perspectives on Modern Persian Literature*, ed. Thomas M. Ricks (Washington D.C.: Three Continents, 1984) 132.

Iranian audience can be interpreted in the light of what Edward Said has called the participation of the modern Orient in its own "orientalizing." In this case, by neglecting a level of Orientalist commentary, i.e. Morier's generalizations regarding the Persian character, Iranians would appear to have adopted the Western stereotypes as true national traits. It is, however, more likely that the Persian readers internalized the exoticism of the original and became fascinated by the possibility of self-examination.

One must also take into account the function served by the Persian translation of Morier's novel in the evolution of Persian literature. That most Persian readers are not aware of the existence of an original text in English would seem to demonstrate the agility of the translator. The Persian text is, in fact, more commonly regarded as an adaptation than a translation:

> In his description of court manners, his exposure of *mullahs*, dervishes, and so on, and with his own additions, the translator has in fact made the Persian text much more subtle and funny than the original. Another great distinction of the Persian edition is the wealth of well-known and proverbial poems that are fitted into appropriate places. This together with a multitude of popular, everyday sayings and the frequent verses quoted from the Koran and the Traditions, indicates the translator's mastery of Persia's literature, life, and language, as well as his knowledge of Islamic institutions.[19]

Moreover, what has served as a source of influence is the prose style of the translation, not that of the original. Morier's text, when translated, came to play a significant role, beyond the intentions of its author, in the history of Persian prose fiction. Along with other models, it provided stimulus for change in the highly ornate prose style of the time. The issue, therefore, goes beyond the supposed superiority of European literature or the inferiority of Persian literature, and points to the inherent complexity of all matters pertaining to cultural interference or exchange.

The prototype of the nineteenth-century representations of the West is

---

[19] Hassan Kamshad, *Modern Persian Prose Literature* (Cambridge: University Press, 1966) 26.

the travelogue. The first generation of Eastern travellers had come to the West often as official emissaries and were escorted through European countries so as to receive a favourable impression. They only saw what was carefully selected for their view; there is little doubt that European states relied on these representatives and their opinion of the West to advocate closer ties between Europe and the Orient. In the later phases of contact, Oriental travellers and immigrants, particularly those coming from European colonies, no longer witnessed a carefully selected, even censored view of Europe, nor did they always find themselves welcome. As a result, they became more intensely drawn into personal assessment and creative response.

One example of this transition is the Egyptian writer Tāhā Husain's autobiographical account of his experiences in Europe, *A Passage to France*.[20] This work forms part three of Tāhā Husain's autobiography and concentrates on that period of the author's life which takes him from Egypt to France (1910–1922). Although *Al-Ayyām* is intended as an autobiography, it is not written in the first person. Instead, the author refers to himself either in the third person or as "our friend."[21] As an attempt to distinguish between the author and the character, as seen in the different stages of his development, this device also signals to the reader some of the psychological effects of Tāhā Husain's physical handicap, i.e. blindness.[22] Having lost his eyesight at an early age, he felt irrevocably distanced from the outside world. In the first volume of his autobiography, he writes of his childhood:

> ... he perceived that other people had an advantage over him and that his brothers and sisters had an advantage over him and that his brothers and sisters were able to tackle things that he could not. He felt that his mother permitted his brothers and sisters to do things that were forbidden to him.

---

[20] The original title is *Al-Ayyām*. The title, *A Passage to France*, has been adopted by the English translator of the third volume.

[21] There are a few instances in which the first person singular is used.

[22] Fedwa Malti-Douglas argues that in *Al-Ayyām*, "Blindness operates as a type of discourse (in the Foucaltian sense) through which the autobiography is conceived and articulated. It is a special vision through which various aspects of the text manifest themselves. It affects the nature of the narrator, and is both central to the act of writing and operative in the creation of a special type of rhetoric." *Autobiography and Blindness: Al-Ayyām of Tāhā Husayn* (Princeton: University Press, 1988) 16.

This aroused, at first, a feeling of resentment, but ere long this feeling of resentment turned to a silent, but heartfelt, grief—when he heard his brothers and sisters describing things about which he had no knowledge at all. Then he knew that they saw what he did not see.[23]

In the English translation of the third volume, the translator has opted for the first-person narrative voice. This change in narrative perspective alters the tone of the original and suggests a different impression of the relationship between the author and the character of the autobiography. As Fedwa Malti-Douglas has demonstrated, the distinct voices in *Al-Ayyām* maintain levels of deliberate ambiguity:

> The narrator operates as a different character from the protagonist, whom he claims to know. Furthermore, it has also become clear that this narrator is sighted, as shown by his power of physical description. The narrator, in addition, does not bestow a proper name on his protagonist, though the text is not altogether devoid of proper names for other characters. What this indicates is that the narrator is the sighted alter ego of the blind protagonist. (111)

Kenneth Cragg justifies his use of the simplified narrative voice by stating: "This English version takes the liberty to make Tāhā Husain speak with the pronoun 'I.' Any other course would seem stilted."[24] Although his choice obscures the ambiguity of the original,[25] it still allows the reader a glimpse of other tensions in the character of the narrator.

In the earlier chapters of *A Passage to France*, the character representing the young Tāhā Husain is eager to depart for France to continue his education. Having undergone a somewhat turbulent career in al-Azhar, the most renowned centre of Islamic learning, followed by a course of study in the newly-established secular Egyptian University, he believes that further development is possible only in the West—this in spite of his

---

[23] *An Egyptian Childhood*, trans. E. H. Paxton (Washington D.C.: Three Continents, 1981) 8.

[24] Tāhā Husain, *A Passage to France*, Arabic Translation Series, 4, trans. Kenneth Cragg (Leiden: E. J. Brill, 1976) XIV.

[25] Malti-Douglas points out: "The sighted narrator is a ruse on the part of a blind author to bypass his handicap in the text when he desires. It permits him to indulge in the process of writing (*écriture*) as though he were sighted, and calls into question his very identity as one who is visually handicapped." (112)

conviction that his education in Egypt has been crucial in reinforcing his identity as a Muslim, especially in the light of his deep appreciation of the West:

> [The Egyptian professors] strengthened and established my Arab, Egyptian personality, in the context of all the wide learning brought to me by the Orientalists which could easily have engrossed me totally in European values. But these Egyptian teachers enabled me to cling to a strong element of authentic eastern culture, and to hold together congenially in a balanced harmony the learning of both east and west. (38)

This harmony becomes precarious when he arrives in France where he begins to doubt the adequacy of his earlier training: "As soon as I embarked on historical and literary studies at the Sorbonne, I realised how ill-prepared I was for them . . . My long apprenticeship in the Azhar and the University had not equipped me for them" (104). This unexpected imbalance between "East" and "West," as two cultural spheres, is at least superficially corrected through the narrator's achievements within the French academic system. He proves to himself that there are no intrinsic reasons for a sustained sense of inferiority, although he continues to regard his French mentors with a reverence he generally begrudges his Egyptian teachers.

Although the distanced tone of the autobiography does not invite speculation on the deeper psychological effects of the narrator's life in France, there are hints of an alienation which pierce even through the controlled narrative: "I was a stranger in my homeland and I was a stranger in France. The life of the people around me left me isolated in mere externalities which hardly mattered or profited . . . People and things were alike a sort of negation. I even doubted my own self and questioned whether I really existed at all" (111–12). This isolation, however, is not specific to France. On the contrary, it is in France that the narrator begins to emerge from his self-imposed exile. Having once chosen the blind poet al-Ma'ari as his spiritual guide, he now turns to his new source of inspiration, "the sweet voice," his fiancée and later his wife. This turning point in the life of the narrator facilitates his crossing of cultures. In the words of Malti-Douglas: "The hero conquers his blindness, as he conquers the West" (88). This personal victory gradually becomes equated with the possibility of an unproblematic synthesis of East and West—a vision which determines the tone of the rest of the narrative. He was to adhere to this conviction throughout his life. Both his private life and his public career became a battleground for this philosophy of cultural harmony. Although he was often criticized, he did not cease to advocate views such as those expressed in *The Future of Culture in Egypt*:[26]

> We must erase from the hearts of Egyptians, individually and collectively, the criminal, the abominable misconception which causes them to imagine that they have been created of a different clay from that of the Europeans, have been compounded of different temperaments from those of Europeans, have been given different minds from those of Europeans.[27]

In the same spirit, he declared Egypt and the entire Arab world part of the larger Western civilization and even encouraged Egyptians "to imitate the methods of the Westerners in order to equal them and to share in their civilization, its goodness and its badness, its sweetness and its bitterness, its beauty and its ugliness, its praiseworthiness and its blameworthiness."[28] At the same time, he continued to promote Arab intellectual independence in both Eastern and Western traditions. His own controversial work on pre-Islamic poetry (*Fī al-Adab al-Jāhilī*), in which he challenged the authenticity of that sacred tradition, was aimed at gaining such stature.[29] The contradictory nature of the two positions he advocated seems not to have been apparent to him.[30] Similar contradictions also haunted Tāhā Husain's personal life.

His own marriage to a Frenchwoman necessitated a modification of his earlier belief that European spouses would undermine and endanger the identity of Muslim men. Yet, his own wife's presence in the autobiogra-

---

[26] *Mustaqbal al-Thaqāfal fī Misr* (Cairo, 1938), translated by Sidney Glazer in 1954.

[27] Quoted by Pierre Cachia in *Tāhā Husayn: His Place in the Egyptian Literary Renaissance* (London: Luzac, 1956) 89.

[28] Quoted by J. Brugman in *An Introduction to the History of Modern Arabic Literature in Egypt* (Leiden: E. J. Brill, 1984) 364–65.

[29] The reception of this book in Egypt is in many ways reminiscent of the fate of Salman Rushdie's *The Satanic Verses* in the Muslim world.

[30] David Semah also argues that the evolution of Tāhā Husain's thought was not without contradictions. See Part Three of *Four Egyptian Literary Critics* (Leiden: E. J. Brill, 1974) 109–52.

phy is limited to references to the nameless author of "that sweet voice." The abstention from a better portrayal of this central figure is, on the one hand, an extension of the narrative distance which Tāhā Husain consistently applies to all levels of personal experience. On the other hand, it is an effective way of balancing the Eastern and Western sources of influence in his life.

There is an obvious degree of artificiality in Tāhā Husain's treatises on the convergence of cultures. His intellectual abstractions, as we have seen, were not always consistent; he seemed to have never fully convinced himself of the concepts he advocated. Even his autobiography, despite its impersonal tone, cannot disguise the ruminations of a divided mind.

The anxiety which is suppressed in *A Passage to France* becomes much more apparent in Tāhā Husain's epistolary novel, *Adīb* (1935). The protagonist, an Egyptian student in Paris, is forced to repudiate his wife in order to qualify for a scholarship abroad. In his letters to a friend at al-Azhar he reveals his uneasy adjustments to life in the West. Although the novel has never been favourably received by critics, in its treatment of cross-cultural dilemmas it is an interesting example of Tāhā Husain's less often articulated apprehensions. It would seem that, despite his desire to bring about a synthesis of East and West, Tāhā Husain was aware of the difficulty of the task he had set for himself. The contradictions he was unable to resolve in his autobiography became less menacing in his scholarly work so that he was able to project the image of a cultural conciliator:

> ... he was launched on a vigorous career in the course of which—by dint of challenge, exhortation, and example—he provided Arab Modernism with its most appealing formulation: not Innovation but Renovation, the revitalization of a great cultural heritage by bringing the best modes of Western thinking to bear upon it, and this in emulation of forefathers who, in the heyday of Islam, had drawn freely on the resources of Greek civilization.[31]

The Iraqi-born writer Naïm Kattan echoes some of these preoccupations in a much later work, *Adieu Babylone*, a semi-autobiographical

---

[31] Pierre Cachia, "Introduction to *An Egyptian Childhood*." No pagination is provided in the Introduction.

account of a first encounter with the West. The mixture of fiction and autobiography leads Kattan to a level of distance, as in Tāhā Husain's autobiography, which reveals itself in the namelessness of the protagonist. For Kattan, and by extension the nameless protagonist of his novel, however, the clash of cultures begins before the departure for the West.

Born into a Jewish community in predominantly Muslim Iraq, Kattan was educated in Arabic as well as Hebrew and French and English, but even early in his youth he closely identified with Arab literature and culture. After studying at the Law College of Baghdad, he attended the Sorbonne and obtained a degree in literature. In 1954 he emigrated to Canada where he has adopted, almost instinctively, the identity of the "mediating minority." With ease he has maneuvered between the French and the English; while at home in French Canada (he now writes and publishes exclusively in French), he has not divorced himself from English Canada. The traces of Kattan's affinity for French are, as he himself points out, to be found in an earlier phase of his life:

> J'avais le choix entre le français et l'anglais comme deuxième langue, c'était à parité. J'apprenais autant l'anglais que le français et j'ai choisi le français parce que pour moi l'Occident libérateur était francophone. La France était le pays qui me libérait. Quand je commençais à lire les Français, je trouvais tout. Je cherchais évidemment, ce que je cherchais je le trouvais dans la littérature française. Tout ce que je voulais de libérateur, je le trouvais dans cette littérature-là.[32]

To some extent, Kattan's perception of France is similar to Tāhā Husain's on the eve of his departure for that country. In his preface to Kattan's novel, Michel Tournier has drawn parallels between the experiences of the two authors: "On songe à une aventure analogue, trente ans plus tôt, celle du jeune étudiant aveugle Tāhā Hussein, enfermé, au Caire dans les murs d'El Hazar, et luttant lui aussi pour sa libération, pour 'gagner' la France aux deux sens du mot."[33] But unlike Tāhā Husain, Kattan's position vis-à-vis French culture has evolved in the course of his life in the West; witness the deliberate choice to pursue his career in Quebec.

---

[32] Jacques Allard, "Entrevue avec Naïm Kattan," *Voix et Images* 11 (1985): 13.
[33] Michel Tournier, "Préface à *Adieu Babylone*" (Paris: Juillard, 1976) IV.

He was drawn to Quebec for the possibility it offered him of being positioned on the borders of many identities. Moreover, French Canada served as an analogy for the life of the Jewish minority in Iraq. Kattan's understanding of the frustrations of a cultural group forced onto the margins of society made him sympathetic towards French Canada, and by adding his voice to that of French-Canadian writers, Kattan has become an encouraging reminder of the possibility of emerging from the periphery.[34] In an essay on the dilemma of the French-Canadian writer, Kattan alludes to his grasp of these writers' need to speak in their own voice:

> Pour prendre la mesure d'une réalité qu'il tente de saisir avant de l'assumer, le romancier du Québec doit inventer un langage et, en s'écartant de la tradition française, prendre le risque de réduire son propos à une attitude, un geste, une prise de position qui l'enferment dans une voie sans issue.[35]

It is because of the facility with which he moves in and out of the confines of cultures that Naïm Kattan has been able to fit so easily into the Canadian mosaic.[36] Reciprocally French and English Canadians, alike, have accepted Kattan as the very model of the cross-cultural man. The following titles from reviews of Kattan's works underline the novelty that Kattan, as a phenomenon, has introduced into Canadian life: "Our only Arab-Jewish-French-Canadian Writer,"[37] and "Bridge of Tongues: Why an Arabic-speaking, Baghdad-born Jew is a Perfect Guide to the Modern Canadian Experience."[38] The most insightful description of Kattan's unique and deliberate position at the crossroads of many

---

[34] "Kattan's stories are refreshing in that they don't follow the mainstream of Quebec's nationalism. From him we learn the solitude of the minorities of a minority. Social integration into the Canadian society is a very difficult thing. But, paradoxically, the loneliness and the isolation of Kattan's characters make them rather similar to the other heroes of contemporary Quebec literature." Alexandre Amprimoz, "Quebec Writers: The Anatomy of Solitude," *The Tamarack Review* 72 (Fall 1977): 82.

[35] Naïm Kattan, "Littérature de [sic] Québec: langue et identité," *Canadian Literature* 58 (Autumn 1973): 61.

[36] "I'm not Canadian just because I *prefer* Canada to the United States . . . I have become part of the ethos of what is Canada." Quoted by Wayne Grady in "The Other Canadian," *Books in Canada* 11.5 (1982): 9.

[37] *Saturday Night* 1 (1979): 9.

[38] I. M. Owen, *Books in Canada* 5.12 (1976): 5.

cultures has come from Jacques Allard in the preface to his interview with Kattan:

> ... un voyageur du transculturel, soucieux de comprendre les rapports de l'Orient et de l'Occident et tout aussi bien ceux des groupes ethniques canadiens. Juif d'Arabie, Arabe de la judéité, oriental d'Occident, occidental d'Orient, l'homme de Bagdad est inépinglable; ce francophone québécois est toujours ailleurs que là où on le fixe quand on ne veut pas comprendre la richesse du désert sémitique originel. Et son discours: celui du migrant, fatalement.[39]

Kattan's predilection for a precarious existence is also reflected in his first novel. The plot concerns the life and education of a Jewish Iraqi youth who, like the author, receives a scholarship to continue his studies in France. *Adieu Babylone* could be seen as an autobiographical *Bildungsroman*, what one reviewer describes as "a kind of Iraqi *Portrait of the Artist as a Young Man*."[40] There are enough obvious parallels between the nameless protagonist of *Adieu Babylone* and Kattan that an autobiographic pact[41] between the author and the reader can be taken for granted. In the interview with Allard, Kattan himself confirms the existence of an autobiographical dimension in his novel:

> Ce que j'avais transporté en moi, je voulais le transmettre. Mais je ne voulais pas le transmettre comme document, je voulais le transmettre comme ce qui était une mémoire vivante et ce qui n'était pas mort était là. Ce ne pouvait être qu'un roman. Donc il y a beaucoup de choses qui ne sont pas documentées mais qui sont pour moi réelles et vraies. (14)

In another instance Kattan speaks of the place of autobiography in his poetics of the novel: "I write novels, which are direct chronicles of ordinary life, mainly reminiscences that have some kind of autobiographical base."[42]

---

[39] J. Allard, "Naïm Kattan ou la fortune du migrant," *Voix et Images* 11 (1985): 7.

[40] Anthony Appenzell, "The Modes of Maturity," *Canadian Literature* 72 (Spring 1977): 72.

[41] Philippe Lejeune argues that the genre of autobiography need not be limited to the cases in which there is explicit reference to the identity of the author. Instead, it is the existence of a "pact" or an understanding between the reader and the author which determines the limits of the genre. *Le Pacte autobiographique* (Paris: Seuil, 1975), section 1, "Le Pacte."

[42] Qtd. in Grady 10.

The two novels written after *Adieu Babylone*, *Les Fruits arrachés* and *La Fiancée promise*, are also autobiographical in nature. Together they form a cycle which traces the life of a young Jewish Iraqi from Baghdad to Paris and Montreal.

Behind the opening scene of *Adieu Babylone* there is a subtle effort to paint an image of the Iraqi society as an integrated whole; we witness a gathering of students from widely disparate cultural and linguistic groups who, regardless of their differences, engage in discussions: "Dans notre groupe, nous n'étions ni Juifs ni Musulmans. Nous étions Irakiens, soucieux de l'avenir de notre pays, par conséquent de notre avenir à chacun de nous."[43] Nevertheless, there is a sense of tension conveyed both in the dialogues and the descriptions. Names and racial designations become almost interchangeable and there develops a rivalry between two camps: "A la fin de la soirée, la partie était gagnée. Pour la première fois, des Musulmans nous écoutaient avec respect. Nous étions dignes de notre dialecte . . . Et en pur dialecte juif nous dressons les plans d'avenir de la culture irakienne" (13). With this statement the protagonist admits to being an outsider in his own country.

Over this opening scene and, in fact, over the entire narrative hangs the novel's biblical epigraph which serves as a reminder of the sense of confinement experienced by the protagonist: "Nabucadnestar emmena captifs à Babylone ceux qui échappèrent à l'épée; et ils lui assujettis à lui et à ses fils" (9). Iraq, even as a homeland, is a symbol of incarceration; hence, the "Babylone" of the title. Disheartened by the strife in his immediate surroundings, the narrator grasps for an alternative. Through his readings of Western literature, he creates a utopian image of the West and looks towards it for the possibility of escape: "Un monde nouveau surgissait devant moi. La lointaine Europe prenait forme. Dans les romans, les femmes étaient réelles. Les hommes leur parlaient, les regardaient vivre, marcher au grand jour, exprimer leur volonté ouvertement" (81). Given his longing for the "exotic," he develops a naïve admiration for Europeans. In his first encounter with a Frenchman he is awestruck, for he sees the Frenchman as an embodiment of all that he admires in the West: "Je regardais avec des yeux avides mon examin-

---

[43] Naïm Kattan, *Adieu Babylone* (Montréal: La Presse, 1975) 12.

ateur: c'était le premier Français authentique que je voyais en chair et en os" (133). However, his ideals are quickly shattered as the image of the Frenchman begins to jar with reality. He is astonished by his French instructor's disinterest in Middle Eastern literature: "Quelle ne fut pas ma déception quand, parlant avec enthousiasme de Gibran, mon professeur de français m'avoua sans honte qu'il n'en avait jamais entendu parler" (82). This realization draws him closer to his Arab heritage. His ideals are even more deeply challenged in the course of an interview with a French official who, in rejecting his application for a government scholarship, reveals that the French benevolence towards Iraq is only a means of gaining control over the country: "La France veut conserver son influence dans le Moyen Orient. Elle a besoin de former de futurs alliés qui la défendraient. Toi, tu es juif. Tu feras tes études en France. Tu réussiras et tu ne rentreras pas" (230).

This event marks a turning point in the life of the protagonist; he recognizes that his own image of the French, ideal as it may have been, was not essentially different from the French stereotypes of the Arab. Both attitudes stem from the same reductive reasoning which forces his own community to exist on the margins of Iraqi society and to be eternally regarded as a minority. His experiences in France further reinforce these views, for he continues to suffer from stereotyping. His response to this treatment becomes much more articulate in the second novel, *Les Fruits arrachés*. Recalling a conversation with Albert Béguin, he reflects on his fate in Paris:

> Pourquoi faut-il qu'on reconnaisse les véritables traits de mon visage, qu'on me définisse? Cette ombre qui m'entoure, qui recouvre ma silhouette, n'est-ce pas la mesure de ma liberté, le prix qu'il faut payer pour que cette liberté ne soit pas délimitée, encadrée, encagée?[44]

The protagonists' encounter with the West, therefore, further distances him from the utopian visions of his youth. The flight from Iraq marks a new beginning which not only does not erase the past but also cannot promise, especially in the light of the second novel, a resolution to the dilemma of the cultural wanderer. Yet this journey away from

---

[44] Naïm Kattan, *Les Fruits arrachés* (Montréal: Hurtubise, 1977) 177.

Babylon, as a symbol of subjugation, enables the protagonist to create and preserve an imaginative past that will continually be integrated with his experience of other cultures:

> Ces visages qui me regardent, qui s'éloignent, que je regarde à travers la fenêtre de l'autobus, ce sera l'Irak. Tout ce qui m'en restera. Pourvu que je puisse en emporter à jamais, en moi le dernier reflet. Il le fallait. Ainsi mon enfance sera préservée, je ferai mon entrée dans le monde nouveau sans m'amputer d'une part privilégiée, sans disperser en pure geste ce morceau de rêves et de souvenirs. (237)

For Naïm Kattan and for his protagonists, who are fragments of his own personality, the West is equated with a liberating force within. Westward migration, as depicted in *Adieu Babylone* and enacted in Kattan's life, is a symbolic embracing of a manifold identity, bound by neither East nor West. Kattan's concerns—and those of many Eastern writers—reach beyond real or imaginary distinctions between East and West. They are implicitly and sometimes explicitly a confirmation of the complexity and multi-dimensionality of all cultures:

> Sommé de s'identifier, il fait l'inventaire des mondes et des cultures auxquels il se rattache, non pour trouver une univocité du je qui ne pourrait être qu'artificielle mais pour prendre en compte sa complexité et en accepter les contradictions. La structure même des romans reflète très bien cette démarche tout comme leur contenu thématique renvoie aux sources mêmes de l'écriture katannienne.[45]

Like Ṭāhā Husain, Naïm Kattan celebrates all juxtapositions of East and West. In contrast to Ṭāhā Husain, however, he does not envision a synthesis but rather an everlasting process of conflation.

In his novel *Les Boucs*, the Moroccan writer Driss Chraïbi presents confrontation as the only means through which East and West can meet. Although the novel belongs to an earlier phase of Chraïbi's career, in a postface written twenty years after the first publication of the novel, he still holds to the convictions which motivated the creation of his work:

> La question m'a été posée—et je me la suis posée: suis-je encore capable, vingt ans après, d'en écrire un tel livre, aussi atroce? Il m'est difficile d'y

---

[45] Sylvain Simard, "Naïm Kattan: la promesse du temps retrouvé," *Voix et Images* 11 (1985): 30.

répondre, sinon par une autre question: vingt ans après, le racisme existe-il encore en France? Les immigrés qui continuent de venir travailler dans ce pays "hautement civilisé" sont-ils encore parqués à la lisière de la société et de l'humain? Est-il toujours vrai, selon mon maître Camus, que la bacille de la peste ne meurt ni ne disparaît jamais?[46]

There are no idealized images of the West in Chraïbi's novel. For the protagonist, Yalaan Waldik,[47] an aspiring Algerian writer, the West represents rejection, suffering, and alienation. After his arrival in France, that is after the initial entrapment in the vision of the colonizer, he no longer sees the West as an ideal refuge. The Berber shoeshine boy, who believes a French priest's promise of hope and gives up all of his possessions to leave for France, realizes that for the French he will always remain an imitator of their civilization:

> Mac n'a peut-être rien dit de tout cela. N'en a même rien pensé. Mais je l'entendais: Il ne travaille même pas, disait-il. Il prend ses désirs pour des réalités; j'ai souvent relu ses lettres. Le cas typique d'un intellectuel ou plutôt d'un néo-intellectuel venant d'un autre continent, d'une autre somme d'histoire. Maniant avec quelque aisance notre langue et nos avocasseries européenes, mais uniquement cela . . . il a la prétention, l'ambition, la naïveté de vouloir (ses lettres le dénotent clairement) imposer l'Orient en Europe. (75–6)

In France even his most intimate relationships are determined by the set of stereotypes which have encompassed all North Africans. His French lover, Simone, cannot see him outside the framework of these stereotypes. Her hatred of North Africans is an instinctive reaction which strips her of her humanity:

> Aux commissures de ses lèvres il y avait un filet d'écume et je la vis telle qu'en elle-même la nature la changeait—tares, avatars, éducation, civilisation, refoulements, quinze siècles de suprématie européene, tout s'était englouti en un instant—une bonne vieille haine exempte du brimborions: chair, organes, instincts. (44)

It is the same instinct which reduces the plight of North Africans in France to what Waldik with irony describes as "twenty thousand tons of suffering." By speaking on their behalf, Waldik assumes the role of a

---

[46] Driss Chraïbi, *Les Boucs* (Paris: Denoël, 1976) 195.
[47] The name literally means, "May he who sired you be damned."

representative. It is as if, through the act of writing, he hopes to bridge the gap between the two sides. Yet the rejection of his manuscript by the French editor, which further reduces him to a type, makes his task impossible. As Waldik fails to establish new channels of communication, the fate of North Africans in France remains unchanged. This is mirrored in the last episode of the novel, which describes the meeting between the Berber and the French priest. In this scene Chraïbi sets up a nefarious infinity of mirrors which imitates the course of history:

> Un petit Berbère cirait des souliers à Bône. Ils étaient noirs et appartenaient à un prêtre. —Comment t'appelles-tu? lui demanda le prêtre. —Yalaan Waldik, dit le Berbère. —Que fais-tu et quel âge as-tu, mon enfant? —Je suis cireur et j'ai dix ans. Le prêtre poussa un soupir . . . —Considère, mon enfant, dit-il. Si tu étais en France, tu apprendrais déjà le latin et le grec et dans dix ans tu serais un homme. Longtemps, le petit Berbère le regarda, stupéfait . . il ferma sa boîte de cireur comme on ferme la porte d'un passé—et s'en alla . . . Et le prêtre dit à voix haute: —J'ai sauvé une âme. (193–4)

What is laid bare in this passage is not only the fallacy of the *mission civilisatrice* but also the naïveté of the North Africans. Seduced by false promises, they are equally blamed for the fate they suffer in France.[48] This does not diminish the responsibility of the colonizer who stubbornly refuses to admit to defeat. The French society's refusal to come to terms with the North African dilemma is, in Chraïbi's view, a reflection of their inability to recognize their own failures.

In Chraïbi's novel, coming to terms with the West is not merely represented by an effort to maintain a position between two worlds but also by a bitter struggle for daily survival. Chraïbi's disgust with the French treatment of the inhabitants of their former North African colonies is crudely, but perhaps most effectively, expressed in the description of a meal of fried mice and rats shared by Waldik and Raus. The anger and the violence of *Les Boucs*, directed towards Europe, is to some extent the outward expression of the tensions present in the preceding

---

[48] Similar sentiments are reflected in Isabelle's remarks to Waldik: "-Exploitation de l'Arabe par l'Européen, oui martela-t-elle avec un rire aigu. Je le condamne certes . . . Oui j'ai honte d'être une Européenne—Mais c'est vous, Nord-Africains, que je condamne le plus. Parce que vous vous êtes toujours laissés faire." (181)

works. In an interview Chraïbi reiterates the necessity of bridging cultural gaps: "J'ai la fierté, de vouloir réussir là où les politiques se sont cassé les dents, c'est-à-dire établir un pont entre deux cultures."[49] If Yalaan Waldik is the author's alter ego, his task must remain open-ended; his text is a step towards eliminating the type of confrontations which dictate the tone of his presentation. However, confrontation must not necessarily be seen in an unfavourable light; it can, as Chraïbi indicates, also lead to certain forms of recognition.

In travelogue, autobiography, and fiction we have seen the West portrayed as an object of an imaginative longing, a haven for intellectual development, a threat to one's identity, and the locus of most bitter disappointments. In other words, there does not exist in these works a singular "image" of the West, unlike the "Orient" Western writers have, at least according to Said, posited. This is far from saying that stereotyping does not exist in the East. Nor is it possible to suggest that those Easterners who are aware of having been perceived as "Oriental subjects" are less inclined towards stereotyping others within their own culture. In some instances, as in the case of Oriental women, those same "subjects" appear to have fully and indiscriminately internalized Western attitudes towards their own societies.

---

[49] Lionel Dubois, "Interview de Driss Chraïbi," *Revue Celfan Review* 5.2 (1986): 21.

Chapter Two
A Double Dilemma: Oriental Women's Encounter with the West

> Und die Frauen,
> Unsere Frauen:
> mit ihren unheimlichen und glücklichen Händen,
> mit ihren zierlichen, kleinen Kinnen, ihren großen
> Augen, unsere Mutter, unser Weib, unsere Geliebte
> Frauen, die sterben, ohne daß sie gelebt hätten.[1]
>
> (Nazim Hikmet)

That the experience of Oriental women in the West needs to be treated separately might at first seem unjustified, for the Western image of the East encompasses men and women alike. But traditionally Oriental women have been subjected to an even more demeaning set of stereotypes. We need only recall a figure such as Flaubert's Kuchuk Hanem to confirm that Oriental women are particularly vulnerable to the Orientalist vision of the East. In *Orientalism*, Edward Said has argued that the Orientalists' treatment of Eastern women has always been integral to the very logic of their discourse:

> Orientalism itself . . . was an exclusively male province; like so many professional guilds during the modern period, it viewed itself and its subject matter with sexist blinders. This is especially evident in the writing of travelers and novelists: women are usually the creatures of a male power-fantasy. They express unlimited sensuality, they are more or less stupid, and above all they are willing. (207)

This interdependence of the sexist and the Orientalist perspectives has been further explored by Rana Kabbani in *Europe's Myths of Orient*. In the

---

[1] Quoted in Saliha Scheinhardt's *Frauen, die sterben, ohne daß sie gelebt hätten* (Berlin: EXpress, 1983) 21–2.

image of the Orient projected in the Victorian era, Kabbani detects the patriarchal tendencies of contemporary European societies: "Although there were notable instances of Victorian women who travelled and wrote about the lands they passed through or took up residence in, the very essence of Victorian travel writing remains an intrinsic part of patriarchal discourse" (7). The Victorian male encounter of the East was at once an exercise of power and a form of outlet from the sexual taboos of the time. Like Said, Kabbani sees an obvious link between sexist and Orientalist discourse; the myth of a sensual Orient was used as an effective vehicle for subduing and dominating the East:

> All Easterners were ultimately dependent in the colonial power balance, but women and young boys especially so. Thus they served as the colonial world's sex symbols, its accomodating objects. Since the Victorian imagination could not conceive of female eroticism divorced from female servitude; since in the core of nineteenth-century sexuality there lurked all the conflicts of power and powerlessness, wealth and poverty, mastery and slavehood, the spectacle of subject women (and boys) could not but be exciting. (80–81)

Kabbani's discussion of the relationship between power and sexuality, however, becomes obscured as she devotes herself to cataloguing the incidents of this image of the Orient and overlooks the significance of some of the examples she has selected. For instance, the intermingling of sexuality and violence in a pictorial representation like Eugène Delacroix's "La Mort de Sardanapale" could be studied as an emblem for Europe's self-projections as well as stereotypical depictions of the East. In such paintings, the European is posited at once as the creator and the observer. While moulding an image of the Orient, albeit unintentionally, the European renders his motivations and desires transparent. This is an extension of the dialectic of the self and the other; the representations of the other can be reversed to provide an inward mirror for the self.

Although Kabbani concentrates on only one dimension of the European image of the East, within it, nevertheless, she finds a "double dilemma:"

> The Orient for Burton was chiefly an illicit space and its women convenient chattels who offered sexual gratification denied in the Victorian home for its

unseemliness. The articulation of sexism in his narrative went hand in hand with the articulation of racism, for women were a sub-group in patriarchal Victorian society just as other races were sub-groups within the colonial enterprise. Oriental women were thus doubly demeaned (as women, and as "Orientals") whilst being curiously sublimated. (7)

The myth of Oriental woman is not to be found only in narratives. The type of distortion to which Kabbani refers[2] also spread to other forms of representation. In *The Colonial Harem*, Malek Alloula studies the representations of Algerian women in postcards dating from a period of French colonial rule in North Africa (1900–1930), and lays bare the implicit meaning of the Orientalist or the colonialist vision. In a range of photographs from veiled women,[3] caught in the course of daily life, to unveiled and finally nude models, posing for the camera[4] Alloula finds the photographer's initial rejection by the very society he sets out to represent and his subsequent attempts at compensation through exaggerated actualizations of his fantasy:

> Draped in the veil that cloaks her to her ankles, the Algerian woman discourages the *scopic desire* (the voyeurism) of the photographer. She is the concrete negation of this desire and thus brings to the photographer confirmation of a triple rejection: the rejection of his desire, of the practice of his "art," and of his place in a milieu that is not his own. (7)

Confronted with these denials, the photographer replaces real figures with easily manipulated models. The result is not only distortions of native life but also attempts to reconfigure Algerian society according to

---

[2] "The *Arabian Nights* was manipulated into an occasion for a sexual discourse, and the tales became valuable as text to be annotated and augmented. From being the *belle dame* of Galland's *salon*, Scheherazade changed into the gay woman of Burton's club, for private subscription only." (36)

[3] "The whiteness of the veil becomes the symbolic equivalent of blindness: a leukoma, a white speck on the eye of the photographer and on his viewfinder. *Whiteness is the absence of a photo, a veiled photograph, a whiteout in technical terms.*" The Colonial Harem, trans. Myrna Godzich and Wlad Godzich, Theory and History of Literature, 21 (Minneapolis: University of Minnesota Press, 1986) 7.

[4] "It is easy to imagine the photographer moving among the models, issuing instructions on posture, and generally improving the group's photographic appearance, which, incidentally, calls to mind the passing in review of the troops so dear to colonial sensibilities." (34)

the norms of the observer. In a chapter entitled "Couples," Alloula demonstrates the way in which the colonizer's conceptions of familial setting are transposed on Algerian families. Disregarding the significance of the extended family, the photographer reproduces portraits of Algerian couples as understood by his European audience. Therefore, he creates "an aberration," "an unthinkable possibility in Algerian society" (38). Alloula sees the act of photographing Algerian couples as more than a careless misunderstanding; carefully arranged in front of the camera, the unrealistic couples "pose" a threat to the very structure of Algerian society.

The representations of the harem fall within the same category of distortion. As depicted by the French photographer, the harem is seen as a "hotbed of sensuality" (86) and lazy passivity. Ironically, at least by Alloula's accounts, it is the photographer himself who becomes a victim of his own unrealizable fantasies: "Voyeurism turns into an obsessive neurosis. The great erotic dream, ebbing from the sad faces of the wage earners in the poses, lets appear, in the flotsam perpetuated by the postcard, another figure: that of *impotence*" (122).

This same logic, in reverse, can be applied to the situation of the Algerians and, by extension, to Alloula's own analysis. A parallel can be drawn between the author of the colonial postcard and his Algerian subjects; on the one hand, as argued by Alloula, the veil of an Algerian woman is a form of protest and a rejection of the gaze of the photographer. On the other hand, however, this same act of rebellion creates another form of internalized colonial submission. If a woman's veil is the only possible means of insurrection for Algerians, they, too, seem powerless vis-à-vis their subjugators. In the final analysis, Algerian men appear to have shared the colonizer/photographer's perspective, for they too considered women their exclusive property. The French colonial photographers obviously relied upon the Algerians to partake of the same perception of women, otherwise they would not have wielded the kind of power Alloula attributes to them. Presumably, an equivalent metaphorical capturing of Algerian men in photographs would not have been desirable or effective. This possibility calls into question the nature of colonial power. If, as it seems, the male Orientals contributed as much as Europeans to the creation of the myth of Oriental woman, then the magnitude of the power exerted by the colonizer is, at least partially, determined by the colonized. In the case of Oriental women and their treatment at the hands of Europeans the Oriental societies are, by no means, to be regarded as powerless.

With this perspective in mind, I wish to redefine Kabbani's "double demeaning" of Oriental women. This term best refers to the simultaneous stereotyping of Oriental women by the West and the East.

Women in the East have spoken against their own cultures' rather primitive view of women. If we allow a momentary digression to examine a few examples which demonstrate Eastern women's plight in their native lands, we will better grasp the "double dilemma" of Oriental women to be studied in texts devoted to their experiences abroad.

In her poem, "Tears", the Syrian poet Saniyya Saleh articulates what is, at least now, recognized as a universal problem for women in all cultures, i.e being excluded from certain realms of society. But what makes her poem particularly interesting for this analysis is its emphasis on the forced suppression of a desire to rebel:

> There is a scream that binds my heart to
> the throat of the Earth
> And that foam is
> my lost voice.
>
> My robe illusion
> My necklace of counterfeit stone
> All that is the world may be
> deceit
> but my tears.
>
> I am the woman bleeding the sharpened years
> I come and go behind
> Tall windows.
> a woman in veils about to flee
> My childhood smashed by this
> nightmare.[5]

The image of the woman behind "tall windows"[6] brings to mind some

---

[5] Kamal Boullata, ed. *Women of the Fertile Crescent: An Anthology of Modern Poetry by Arab Women* (1978; rpt. Washington, D.C.: Three Continents, 1981) 205.

[6] This same image is found in the Egyptian writer Ihsan Kamal's short story, "A

of the representations of women in the French colonial postcards.[7] The context in which Saniyya Saleh's poem was written cannot be directly related to the experience of the colonized Algerian women, yet the recurrence of the same images suggests that there is little difference between the European and the Oriental perception of women.

In her poetry, the Iranian Furugh Farukhzad also defied tradition and voiced her dissatisfaction with the dominant male perspective with which she, as a poet, was required to comply. The very titles of her collection of poems, *Prisoner*, *The Wall*, and *Rebellion*, reflect her sentiments vis-à-vis her tradition. Repeatedly she was chastised for questioning the treatment of women in her society.[8] The following poem, entitled "A Cold Season," was highly criticized even by her contemporaries for its bold and challenging images:

> And this is I
> A lonely woman
> On the threshold of a cold season
> At the beginning of the understanding of the
>   contaminated existence of earth.
> And the simple despair and sadness of sky
> And the weakness of these cemented hands.
>
> On the threshold of a cold season
> In the circles of the mourning of mirrors
> And the mournful society of these pale experiences
> And the sunset being pregnant with the knowledge of
>   silence
> How is it possible to command someone who goes so
>   patient,

Jailhouse of My Own": "I do not know why every time I passed in front of the Hadara prison, when I was a child, a tremor ran through my body, and I was filled with pity for the inmates shut behind those high grim walls. Perhaps it was a foreboding of the twenty years I was to spend in another prison, later on. I had committed no crime, unless it is a crime to marry for which the penalty is a life sentence." In *Arabic Short Stories 1945–1965*, ed. Mahmoud Manzaloui (Cairo: The American University in Cairo Press, 1985) 304.

[7] Chapter three, "Women's Prisons," and the photographs on the following pages: 19, 20, 22–3.

[8] For analysis of Farukhzad's poetry, see Hasan Javadi's "Women in Persian Literature: An Explanatory Study," in *Women and the Family in Iran*, ed. A. Fathi (Leiden: E. J. Brill, 1985) 37–59 and Michael C. Hillmann's *A Lonely Woman: Forugh Farrokhzad and Her Poetry* (Washington D.C.: Three Continents and Mage, 1987).

heavy,
wondering,
to stop.
How is it possible to say to man that he is not
  alive, has never been alive.

Dear stars
Dear cardboard stars
When lies billow in the sky
Then how is it possible to rely on the surahs of
  disgraced prophets?
We, like corpses dead a thousand years, will gather
  together; and then
The sun shall judge the rottenness of our dead bodies.

Salaam, O innocent night
Salaam, O innocent night, you who change the eyes of
  the desert wolves
into the bony pit of faith and trust
And on the side of your brook the spirit of willows
smell the kind spirits of apes
I came from the indifferent world of thoughts, words
  and sounds,
And this world is like the nest of snakes,
And this world is full of the sound of the movement
  of people's feet
that, just as they kiss you,
In their imagination weave your noose.

Look here
How the soul of the one who spoke with the word
and played with the glance
and found comfort with fondling; away from running
on the imaginary scaffold,
has been crucified.

Fortunate corpses
Dejected corpses
Quiet and reflective corpses
Well-countenanced, well-dressed, well-fed corpses
In the stations of certain times
And in the doubtful field of temporary lights
And the lust of buying the rotten fruits of vanity
Oh,

> What people at the crossroad are looking for
>   accidents
> And the sound of the stop whistle
> In the moment that a man must, must, must
> be smashed under the wheel of time
> A man who is passing by the wet trees.[9]

The suppressed cries of Saniyya Saleh's poem find a parallel in the stillness and imposed silence of Farukhzad's "A Cold Season." In the latter, however, alienation threatens to give way to a destructive rage, "a man must, must, must, be smashed." Farukhzad did, in fact, envision the possibility of freeing the "cemented hands." Yet, as she pointed out in interviews,[10] her poetry was not concerned exclusively with the predicament of women but rather called for a change in attitudes which create and reinforce all manner of stereotypes.

One of the most interesting representations of the clash of perspectives between Eastern men and women is to be found in the Lebanese Hanan al-Shaykh's novel *The Story of Zahra*.[11] By presenting the same story from two different points of view, Zahra's and that of her husband, Hanan al-Shaykh brings to light the gulf which separates the two. In chapter four, "The Husband," we see the reasoning which renders Zahra a mere object; her flight from Lebanon to West Africa goes unnoticed by her own family and the suitors eager to find a wife. She is never allowed to escape what others have determined to be her fate:

> I married Zahra without knowing her. When I saw her and heard she was still a spinster, and that she was Hashem's niece, I thought: "Here is a ready-made bride waiting. By marrying her I'll be saved from having to go to Lebanon to look for a wife. I'll save the costs of travel and trousseau, for I've heard that brides here do not expect a trousseau as they do back home."[12]

Absorbed in his own plans for the future, Zahra's husband is therefore oblivious to her already advanced neurosis. For her, what had been an

---

[9] Bahram Jamalpur, trans., *Modern Islamic Literature from 1800 to the Present*, 188–9.
[10] Taped interviews distributed by the Ketab Corporation in Encino, California.
[11] The original text is in Arabic and was first published in Lebanon in 1980.
[12] Hanan al-Shaykh. *The Story of Zahra*, translated by Readers International (London: Readers International, 1986) 61.

attempt to escape becomes a second stage of incarceration. By consenting to the marriage, she once again admits defeat in utter despair. Although only partially aware of her husband's image of herself, she is nevertheless repelled by his physical presence:

> Dear God! The things that I feel whenever Majed comes close to me! Cold winds, cold, crowding me close with thousands of snails crawling closer, crawling across the mud as the winds blow ever more strongly, carrying the snails' foul odour which soaks into every pore. I wanted to live for myself. I wanted my body to be mine alone. I wanted the place on which I stood and the air surrounding me to be mine and no one else's. (78)

What precipitates the breakdown of their marriage is not Zahra's suffering but rather the husband's shame; Zahra's "madness" becomes an embarrassment to him which allows him to discard her. This fate is repeated in her affair after her return to Lebanon. When she ceases to comply with her role as a sexual object, she is to be destroyed: "He's killed me. That's why he kept me there till darkness fell. Maybe he couldn't face pulling the trigger and dropping me to the ground in broad daylight" (183). Zahra's fate reflects that of many women in the East and when transplanted in the West it becomes even more problematic. The promise of freedom in the West, as in Zahra's flight from the homeland, is hardly ever fulfilled. Instead, it often becomes necessary for these women to cope with a new set of hardships.

In her memoirs, the Egyptian playwright and director, Laila Said, stresses some of these dilemmas by juxtaposing her life in Egypt with a period of her career in the United States. It is during her adolescence in Egypt that she recognizes the course of her life to have been predetermined by traditions which give little credence to her own ambitions. A passage in which she recalls an engagement party organized by her own family and that of a suitor underlines the essence of her early experience in Egypt:

> The moment I took my place in the circle, I knew what was happening. Is this how they marry you off? I wondered. There was a soothing breeze which not even the circle which was tightening around me could dispel. I had heard about such events. At school, my girlfriends and I often asked ourselves what we would do when the day came and we were "displayed" how we would behave . . . But who was I being displayed for? Who was

> the man sitting in that affluent circle who would decide that afternoon whether he would have me for his wife? . . . Why was I sitting there, trapped like a helpless animal? Because my parents wanted it? Because the ancient laws of the land required it? Because I was a woman?[13]

Although she does not consent to the role allotted to her and finally breaks off her marriage, her compatriots' perception of her hardly changes; her efforts to revive a national theatrical tradition are ridiculed, at best dismissed as uninteresting: "He did not protest as I launched into my description, but it was clear from the expression on his face that he was humouring me. It was an expression I was to see on the faces of many men—right, left, or center—when I talked about women's rights" (159).

In the course of her education in the United States, she comes across a double barrier. On the one hand, like other Egyptians, she finds Americans unsympathetic towards her concerns: " . . . we [a group of Egyptian students] couldn't find a single paper expressing the Arab viewpoint. We protested to the editors of this or that magazine in long letters, which we were too discouraged even to mail" (63). On the other hand, she finds herself stereotyped as an Oriental woman. Her encounter with two policemen who warn her to stay off the streets is a case in point. It is only a black maid who identifies with her dilemma and serves as a reminder of the ways in which sexism and racism are manifestations of a similar state of mind:

> Grinning, with her gold teeth glinting, she said, "Oh, honey, those white folks are so scared of us. But you have nothin' to worry about . . ." she added with a gesture of her hand, as if to say, you are one of us. I smiled gratefully. "Do they put you down as Caucasian when they ask about your race?" I asked her naively. "No, hon," she replied, "just Negro." (21)

These impressions prepare her for an initiation into feminism. At a much later stage, while on a visit to New York, Laila meets Gloria Steinem and feels herself drawn to an ideology which seems to constitute an alternative to life in Egypt. Her somewhat naïve willingness to be absorbed in this new life is underlined in the description of Gloria

---

[13] Laila Said, *A Bridge Through Time: A Memoir* (New York: Summit, 1985) 12.

Steinem's apartment: "Phylis spoke in muted tones as she showed me around. I followed her about like someone being initiated in a new rite: the feminist religion. For that was the religion worshipped in these two rooms" (212). The irony of this passage becomes obvious as Laila engages in the Western feminists' crusade on behalf of Iranian women. As a member of a delegation of feminists who travel to Iran in 1979, Laila finds herself ill at ease both in the world of the Iranian patriarchy and that of the Western feminists. Ironically, it is in Iran that the discrepancies between these two realms startle her out of her earlier naïveté:

> At dinner I could hardly eat. The other feminists devoured their roasted lamb and rice, but in a few days they would be back in Paris or elsewhere, back to their stable lives, their bistros, their Peugeots, their feminist magazines, their jeans, and their unthreatened lives. In Cairo, I did not know what would greet me. Women there had already started to wear the veil. (223)

She is also forced to acknowledge the existence of Middle Eastern feminist groups whose goals may be at odds with her own. She does not directly address this issue, but in choosing Nawal al-Saadawy's, a well known Egyptian feminist, statement as a heading to the chapter on her visit to Iran she seems to have reached a new and more cynical recognition: "Progressive feminist movements intervened on behalf of Iranian women, not realizing that sometimes the form and content of their intervention was being used to discredit the Iranian people's struggle against American intervention" (221).

Laila Said's recollections, nevertheless, end on a positive note; having witnessed the plight of women in both her own culture and that of Western countries, she begins to see herself in a new light. The recognition that her own fate is inextricably bound to that of other women allows her to overcome cultural barriers and hope for a type of synthesis of East and West otherwise not easily achieved: "Maybe Third World women should not turn down the help they may get from Western women. Maybe we can help one another by holding hands across the barriers of men's ideologies, religions, and political systems in order to find solutions to our common struggles" (281).

No such resolutions are reached in Bharati Mukherjee's[14] novel, *Wife*. The protagonist, Dimple Dasgupta Basu, is portrayed as a naïve Bengali teenager who has been raised to obey what is dictated by the tradition. This entails accepting a husband chosen for her by her elders and becoming a submissive wife. Her acquiescence to this role is suggested in her name, Dimple.[15] After her marriage, she behaves in accordance with the same spirit; she accepts a new name chosen by her mother-in-law.

Only when her husband's plans for emigrating to the United States are postponed, does Dimple become assertive and urge him to act. She sees emigration to the West as a means of escape from her lot in India. For her own part, Dimple tries to remove all obstacles to their departure. She puts an end to her pregnancy, because she perceives it as a hindrance to their move. Furthermore, subconsciously she is repulsed by bearing her husband's child: "She began to think of the baby as unfinished business. It cluttered up the preparation for going abroad. She did not want to carry any relics from her old life" (42). This first step towards determining her own fate sets the tone for the remainder of the novel. The gradual changes in Dimple's character coincide with her arrival in the West and become more problematic in the new setting.

Her friend's prophecy about her future in the West becomes reality, as Dimple finds herself imprisoned in an Indian immigrant colony in New York: "'you may think of it as immigration, my dear, . . . but what you are is a *resident alien*'" (46). There are additional disappointments when she realizes that her idealized images of life in the West clash with the rather mundane details of reality; the sense of irony escapes her, and as a result she sees nothing but her failed quest for the exotic:

> She realized suddenly that she had expected apartments in America to resemble the sets in a Raj Kapoor movie: living rooms in which the guests could break into song and dance, winding carpeted staircases, sunken swimming pools, billiard tables, roulette wheels, baby grand pianos, bars and velvet curtains. (64)

---

[14] Mukherjee was born in India, but has lived most of her life in Canada and the United States.

[15] "A dimple is any slight surface depression." Bharati Mukherjee, *Wife* (Boston: Houghton Mifflin, 1975) epigraph.

Her dreams shattered, Dimple becomes increasingly disenchanted with her husband. With longing, she looks back upon a sheltered and ordered life in India but recognizes that life also to be beyond her grasp. Questioning one culture on the premise of another, she loses her bearings in both:

> It had been better, she decided, on Dr. Sarat Banerjee Road where Amit had been the boss. There she had experienced him in terms of permissions and restraints. Here in New York, Amit seemed to have collapsed inwardly, to have grown frail and shabby. That was the problem: he was shabby compared to the nicely suited Jyoti Sen or the men pushing toothpaste and deodorant on television. She did not trust him anymore, did not trust his high-pitched *yes* and *no* which had once seemed oracular, did not trust his white cotton shirts with erect collars. She wanted Amit to be infallible, intractable, godlike, but with boyish charm. (88–9)

This admission of change in her perception marks the beginning of Dimple's "seduction" by the West. She finds herself more and more drawn towards the so-called westernized Indian women[16] who have rebelled against their traditions. Her daily excursions in the city, her trying out of Western clothing, and finally her affair with Milt Glasser all symbolize her donning of a new identity. These changes, however, do not bring an end to her personal trials. At the crucial moment, Ina Mullick's admission to despair further undermines Dimple's hope of finding an alternative: "'No one—no Bengali, not my husband, not you, absolutely no one understands me. Do you know that last night I thought seriously of suicide? Now do you get it?'" (136). Consequently, Dimple is ever more torn between the images of her past and present: "She felt it was not Dimple Basu who was singing and giggling with Milt Glasser" (194). At the same time, she realizes that in the eyes of this American lover, she will forever be an exotic Oriental woman.

The ending of the novel with its juxtaposition of an outburst of violence and the return, in Dimple's imagination, to the calm composure of an obedient wife sharply underlines the divisions within her personality. Reality and imagination become confused, as she can no longer

---

[16] "Dimple could not take her eyes off Ina Mullick. She was wearing white pants and a printed shirt that ended in a large knot. There was an isosceles triangle of hard flesh between the shirt and the waistband of her pants, with a dimpled navel in the center. Dimple had no idea that skinniness could look so chillingly sexy on some people." (74)

distinguish between the fragments of her identity: "but of course it was her imagination because she was not sure anymore what she had seen on TV and what she had seen in the private screen of three a.m. . . . Women on television got away with murder" (212–13). Her final act of hostility towards Amit is an expression of her frustration with constantly being perceived as a "subject." It is interesting to note, however, that the violence is primarily directed towards her husband, for he represents the world which originally forced her into submission.

Dimple Dasgupta's fate, at least partially, reflects Mukherjee's own cross-cultural dilemmas. As she states in the introduction to a collection of her short stories, Mukherjee herself has suffered stereotyping. Discussing her immigration to the United States, she indicates:

> I had moved from being a "visible minority," against whom the nation had officially incited its less-visible citizens to react, to being just another immigrant. If I may put it in its harshest terms, it would be this: in Canada, I was frequently taken for a prostitute or shoplifter, frequently assumed to be a domestic, praised by astonished auditors that I didn't have a "sing-song" accent. The society itself, or important elements in that society, routinely made crippling assumptions about me, and about my "kind."[17]

Unlike the protagonist of her novel, in the United States Mukherjee has found the means to transcend the issues which in the past troubled her existence in the West.[18] The answer for Mukherjee is, although she does not emphasize this aspect of her personal experience, in her creative works which have granted her a distance from an image of herself, initially influenced by what others saw in her. That self-consciousness has now been sublimated, or at least transformed into a collective dominant identity:

> I have joined imaginative forces with an anonymous, driven, underclass of semi-assimilated Indians with sentimental attachments to a distant homeland but no real desire for permanent return. I see my "immigrant" story replicated in a dozen American cities, and instead of seeing my Indianness as

---

[17] Bharati Mukherjee, *Darkness* (Markham, Ontario: Penguin, 1985) 2–3.
[18] In a personal note, I would like to add that I myself find it difficult to believe that Canadians are more inclined to stereotyping than Americans. I would suggest rather that Mukherjee's experiences in Canada and the United States belong to two different phases of her personal development.

a fragile identity to be preserved against obliteration (or worse, a "visible" disfigurement to be hidden), I see it now as a set of fluid identities to be celebrated. I see myself as an American writer in the tradition of other American writers whose parents or grandparents had passed through Ellis Island. Indianness is now a metaphor, a particular way of partially comprehending the world. (3)

The illusory nature of what Mukherjee assumes to be her new and less troublesome existence is evident in her most recent collection of short stories, *The Middleman*—a compilation and reduction of the immigrant experience in the United States. For a writer hypersensitive to being stereotyped, Mukherjee shows little discretion in her own stereotyping of other nationalities.

The Turkish novelist Saliha Scheinhardt's *Frauen, die sterben ohne daß sie gelebt hätten* has much in common with Mukherjee's *Wife*. The narrative is based on the true accounts[19] of a Turkish woman's experiences in Germany. The diary begins and ends in a German prison where the protagonist, Suna S., is serving a sentence for having murdered her husband. The first-person presentation of Scheinhardt's work renders the narrative much more confessional than Mukherjee's novel: "Dies ist kein Klagelied! Es ist auch nicht die Bedeutung eines schrecklichen Traumes! Dieses ist die Wirklichkeit, die Geschichte meines kurzen Lebens" (23).

Before her arrival in Germany, like Dimple Dasgupta, Suna S. is seduced by the idea of a distant and exotic land which promises to free her from the confines of life in an Anatolian village:

> Wir alle waren neugierig, wir wollten zu gerne mehr über Deutschland wissen. Wir fragten uns: wo liegt dieses Land, das unsere Männer und Frauen in sich hineinsaugt . . . Ich glaube, zu der Zeit stellten sich Millionen Türken diese Frage. Auch ich! Inzwischen sind Jahre vergangen, ich habe es erfahren bis zum bittersten Ende. Nun weiß ich, wo Deutschland liegt, und wie es in Deutschland aussieht. (37)

---

[19] All of Scheinhardt's narratives are well grounded in real events and factual representations. For this reason, some critics label her works mere "documents," but she has said in her own defence: "My first concern is with authenticity. That is why I do my research as if I were going to write a report, and I analyse my conversations in this way." Quoted in "Books Reveal Tribulations of Turkish Women," *The German Tribune* 9 February 1986: 11.

Her image of Germany is determined first by the exile forced upon her by a husband who uses the foreign setting as a licence to mistreat and abuse her and secondly by the alienation she suffers in Germany. Incarcerated in an apartment, she has almost no means of interacting with Germans, hardly speaks the language, and can therefore have no access to the outside world. It is this helplessness which forces her to act alone and put an end to her suffering: "Nun beschloß die Angeklagte, die in ihrer Verzweiflung keinen anderen Ausweg sah, ihren Mann zu töten."[20]

Ironically, it is only in the course of serving her sentence that Suna develops contacts with Germans. This second experience of Germany mirrors the first one; the barriers of language and culture, at first, separate her from others. Feeling rejected both by her Turkish relatives and the German inmates, she becomes insecure about her own identity: "Manchmal schäme ich mich, daß ich eine Türkin bin, ich möchte nicht ausgelegt werden. Darum schaue ich genau die deutschen Frauen an, ich lasse mir alles erklären, damit ich auch nichts falsch mache" (26). Then, as she gradually learns to communicate with German women, she wants to erase her past altogether.

> Ich wollte mich völlig ändern. Ich wollte die Vergangenheit abschütteln, innerlich und äußerlich. Ich fühlte mich außerdem nicht wohl in meinen alten Kleidern. Alles erinnerte mich an meine Vergangenheit. Natürlich haben meine Bekanntschaften mit deutschen Frauen sehr viel ausgemacht. Sie haben mir immer wieder eingeredet, meine Trauer zuende zu bringen und zu lernen, auch im Gefängnis zu leben. (57)

Despite this new bond with German women, especially those who have suffered similar fates, she comes up against another level of rejection. When she appeals to immigration authorities to be granted permission to remain in Germany instead of being deported to Turkey where she faces revenge from her husband's family, she is turned down. She learns that society as a whole perceives her as a threat: "Warum kann ich nicht hier bleiben? Ich habe keinem Deutschen etwas angetan. 'Die Gesetze sagen es so,' sagte die Sozialberaterin, aber die Gesetze machen doch die Menschen, diese Menschen sollen kommen, sie sollen mich sehen und dann, dann werden sie ganz sicher ihre Gesetze ändern" (67).

---

[20] From the court reports in the appendix 81.

The laws which prevent Suna S. from becoming integrated into German society are in essence the same as those that determined her fate in Turkey. In spite of the changes she has undergone, neither society is willing to allow her a new mode of life. Ultimately, the only place in which she feels secure is the prison—a symbol of her entire existence both in Turkey and Germany.

The conclusion of Scheinhardt's narrative leaves the reader to speculate on the fate of the protagonist much in the same way that Mukherjee leaves her readers with an open-ended final passage. This deliberate ambiguity is intended to reach beyond the texts, i.e. *Wife* and *Frauen, die sterben ohne daß sie gelebt hätten*, and to reflect and question presuppositions on the part of all societies.

The permanent exile of Suna S., like that of Gülnaz K. in *Drei Zypressen*, another of Scheinhardt's works, must be understood not as a product of a particular culture, but rather as a universal dilemma. The opening statement of this second work lays bare the tensions which continue to determine Oriental women's difficult relationship to sources of power and authority:

> Ich liebe meinen Mann, ich liebe meinen Vater. Ich liebe meinen Mann wie meinen Vater. Ich verachte meinen Mann und kann es nicht sagen. Er ist ein Mann. Ich hasse meinen Vater und darf es nicht zeigen. Er ist ein Mann. Ich verabscheue den Meister und kann nicht weglaufen. Er ist ein Mann. Dennoch liebe ich meinen Mann, der mich mit der Kraft seines Körpers zu seiner Frau machte. Ich liebe meinen Vater; so muß es sein, sagte man mir. Oder fürchte ich sie alle?[21]

What is implied in this passage is that Oriental women are still reluctant to oppose openly their state of subjugation, be it in the East or in the West. In some instances, as in the case of Algerian or Iranian women who actively took part in a revolution and embraced the promise of change only to be bitterly disappointed, rebellion no longer provides an answer. As the Algerian feminist writer and film maker Assia Djebar points out, there is indeed little evidence of change in such societies: "depuis quelques décennies—au fur et à mesure que triomphe ça et là chaque nationalisme—, on peut se rendre compte qu'à l'intérieur de cet

---

[21] Saliha Scheinhardt, *Drei Zypressen* (Berlin: Express, 1984) 15.

Orient livré à lui-même, l'image de la femme n'est pas perçue autrement par le père, par l'époux et, d'une façon plus trouble, par le frère et le fils."[22]

Given their "double dilemma," however, Oriental women have taken steps to overcome the image carved for them by others. The Egyptian feminist Nawal al-Saadawy, for instance, has directed her challenges towards social institutions: " . . . the movement of liberation of women, or feminist activities, cannot achieve much by only showing interest in changing laws. They must parallel their struggle for changing laws with an even fiercer struggle to change social institutions through which it would be possible to apply these laws."[23] In fictional representations like Mukherjee's *Wife* and in true accounts such as Scheinhardt's *Frauen, die sterben, ohne daß sie gelebt hätten* counterarguments and change seem possible only through physical force. It is interesting to note that these responses are also directed inward; it is the Eastern men who become the object of the most vehement assaults. The Oriental women's encounter with the West only strengthens their resolve to put an end to their subjugation. Like some of their nineteenth-century male counterparts, these women see the West as a vehicle for self-definition. In this sense, the double dilemma of Oriental women fits within the larger context of the dialectic of the self and the other which has so far dominated our discussion. At the same time, this double focus introduces us to new realms of cross-cultural phenomena to which we must now turn to grasp the full range of Eastern experiences in the West.

---

[22] Quoted by Jean Déjeux in *Assia Djebar: romancière algérienne, cinéaste arabe* (Sherbrooke, Québec: Naaman, 1984) 90.
[23] Quoted by Mona Mikhail in *Images of Arab Women: Fact and Fiction* (Washington D.C.: Three Continents, 1979) 43.

Chapter Three

The Voice of the Cross-Cultural Writer

> What is to be done, O Moslems? for I do not recognise myself.
> I am neither Christian, nor Jew, nor Gabr, nor Moslem.
> I am not of the East, nor of the West, nor of the land, nor of the sea;
> I am not of Nature's mint, nor of the circling heavens.[1]
>
> (Shamsi Tabriz)

Examples from travelogues, personal diaries, and fiction in the preceding chapters have provided some insight into the types of dilemmas faced by Easterners in the West. Seeing themselves through the eyes of the West, Indian, Iranian, Egyptian, and Turkish travellers and immigrants have often perceived themselves as outsiders in Western societies. In the case of writers and artists residing in the West there is even a more acute sense of alienation, because they feel their shattered identity to be impinging upon their creativity. In such instances, the "creative voice" naturally reflects the fragmented identity of the artist. We have seen glimpses of this concern in the works of Driss Chraïbi, Tāhā Husain, and Bharati Mukherjee. However, there are other works of fiction and autobiography whose primary focus is the problematic relationship between a writer's dual vision and his or her creation. In this genre, writing itself becomes a form of catharsis—an objectification and outward projection of inner dilemmas.

In *Days and Nights in Calcutta*, Bharati Mukherjee gives expression to such concerns. The work is an autobiographical account of her return to her homeland after fourteen years of absence in North America. The title, "Days and Nights," must be interpreted on many levels. First, it

---

[1] Reynold A. Nicholson, ed. and trans., *Selected Poems from the Divani Shamsi Tabriz* (Cambridge: University Press, 1977) 125.

reflects the joint authorship of Mukherjee and her husband, Clark Blaise and, therefore, the juxtaposed perspectives of the outsider (Blaise) and the insider (Mukherjee). On a more subtle level, however, the title reflects Mukherjee's own internalized double perspective; in her observations of India she is at once a native and an alien.

During her years of absence from India she had realized that her marriage to a non-Hindu man and the pursuit of her career in North America had distanced her from her own traditions. Ironically, however, her visit to India further widens the gulf between her and the country she left behind. She is chastised for having abandoned her caste[2] and is regarded as an outsider.[3] Moreover, in India she is denied the identity she had carefully shaped for herself in North America:

> Prior to this year-long stay in India, I had seen myself as others saw me in Montreal, a brown woman in a white society, different, perhaps even special, but definitely not a part of the majority . . . But in India I am not unique, not even extraordinary. During the year, I began to see how typical my life had actually been, and given the limited options of a woman from my class and from my city, how predictably I had acted in each crisis. (179–80)

On the one hand, she longs for a uniqueness, apparently only granted her in Canada. On the other hand, she wishes to be reintegrated into the India of her past. This wavering between two positions is clearly reflected in Mukherjee's narrative. Throughout the text, in a manner reminiscent of Said's introductory passage in *After the Last Sky*, the narrative voice vacillates between addressing Indians as "us" and "them."

Nowhere is this more apparent than in the description of her encounters with Indian female friends. Despising these women's limited goals and their unflinching commitment to their husbands and children, she

---

[2] " . . . the wife of the man who had invited himself to Montreal would caution me against touching any religious vessels since I was no longer 'full-Brahmin.'" Bharati Mukherjee and Clark Blaise, *Days and Nights in Calcutta* (New York: Doubleday, 1977) 277.
[3] "To my relatives—who accorded me the status of an honorary male by urging me to eat with Clark and the uncles at the first shift at the dining table, instead of on the floor on the second and third shifts with my aunts and girl cousins—I was the embodiment of 'local-girl makes good.' And I was also an intimidating alien." (225)

does not allow for any intimacy during her reunions with them. Treating "their" ambitions with bitter irony, Mukherjee comes perilously close to adopting the "Orientalist" notion of an India lacking self-criticism. Mukherjee's ironic tone would seem to suggest that she has undertaken a study of Indian "womanhood" rather than specific individuals and former acquaintances:

> In Calcutta, being the wife of a socially and professionally prominent man was a full-time career. Being a woman physician not, for them, a preferred alternative. Their careers as housewives (chatelains is almost appropriate) demanded certain skills: managerial shrewdness, physical stamina, diplomacy. Dressing immaculately when they would rather lounge at home, making small talk with visiting dignitaries, taking the wife of a foreign consul to lunch at the Bengal Club, all this was part of their professional duty. (204)

However, Mukherjee pierces through some of the barriers deliberately set up between herself and other Indian women. In spite of her assumed superiority, Mukherjee cannot maintain complete distance from "them." Such uneasy reintegrations remain, nevertheless, transitory and her visit to India ends without obvious resolutions. Yet, she seems to come closer to understanding her permanent expatriation:

> As I prepared to leave for Bombay for the slow flight westward, I realized that for me there would be no more easy consolation through India. The India that I had carried as a talisman against icy Canada had not survived my accidental testings. I would return, of course, but in future visits India would become just another Asian country with too many agonies and too much passion, and I would be another knowledgeable but desolate tourist. (285)

The ramifications of this new attitude are extremely important for Mukherjee's identity as a writer. Towards the end of her autobiographical narrative she reflects on the possibility of preserving aspects of Hindu culture in her own art, but her ruminations on what constitutes that literary and cultural heritage reveal another level of expatriation. In her description of Hindu aesthetics Mukherjee resorts to generalizations easily traceable to Western stereotypes:

> To admit to possessing a Hindu imagination is to admit that my concepts of what constitute a 'story' and of narrative structure are non-causal, non-

> Western. A Hindu writer who believes that God can be a jolly, potbellied creature with an elephant trunk, and who accepts the Hindu elastic time scheme and reincarnation, must necessarily conceive of heroes, of plot and pacing and even paragraphing in ways distinct from those of the average American. (286)

Almost unintentionally, Mukherjee re-asserts one of the many Western "myths of the Orient"; her claim that Oriental concepts of time and narrative have no rational or causal basis is not far from a similar assessment attributed to the fictional Persian narrator of *Hajji Baba of Isphahan*. Like Hajji Baba, Mukherjee appears to be saying, "Indian, as I am, I have overcome the impossibility of writing like a Westerner." At the same time, she consciously rejects the Western image of herself: "But I am not what I want my dust-jacket to suggest I am. Instead, I am anxious and querulous, convinced that every aspect of the writing profession . . . weighs heavily against me because of my visibility as a stereotype" (286). In the end, however, her quest for an authentic voice leads her to a compliance with her Western audience: "Though in my fiction I may now be ready to construct new metaphorical Indians more real to me than the literary stereotypes, I must first persuade North American readers that the stereotypes are also—if only partially—correct" (286). In her concluding pronouncements on the narrative voice best suited to her writing, Mukherjee overlooks her unresolved differences with the Hindu tradition and envisions a simple merging of Eastern thought and Western conventions:

> To me, the problem of voice is the most exciting one. Born in Calcutta and educated initially in Bengali, I now live in Canada and write in English about Indians living in India or in the United States. My aim, then, is to find a voice that will represent the life I know in a manner that is true to my own aesthetic. But my aesthetic has emerged during my education in North America. I am of the first generation of Indian writers to be influenced by American life and fiction . . . My aesthetic, then, must accommodate a decidedly Hindu imagination with an Americanized sense of the craft of fiction. (286)

The harmony which Mukherjee hopes to bring about in her art seems possible in an abstract form. Because of an obsession with seeing herself through the eyes of others, in India and North America she adopts two different roles. Her only solace is, therefore, in the realm of the imagination where there are no doubtful observers: "I am content that my only stability is the portable world of my imagination" (287). For her audiences who see through her disguises, however, she will always speak in an artificial voice.

The autobiographical narrative voice is also a focal point in Salman Rushdie's third novel, *Shame*. He opts for a narrator whose primary function is to comment upon the unreliability of the authorial perspective. At the same time, the narrative voice is intended to reflect the concerns of an author situated between two cultures. The precarious balance between the subjective and the objective perspectives tends to undermine the authenticity of the authorial voice.

What intensifies the conflict between voices representing the author and the narrator is the concept of shame, integral to the plot of the novel:

> Somebody told me yesterday that Arthur Koestler said that the world is divided into two main controlling forces: in the West you have guilt, in the East you have shame, and that these were the things around which the world revolved. And I came to think about this, I've never read this in Koestler, but it seems that if he does say it, he's right. Because shame and its opposite, which is honour, seem to me to be kind of central to the society I was describing, to such an extent that it was impossible to explain the society except by looking at it through these concepts.[4]

On a superficial level, Rushdie is merely contrasting Eastern and Western perceptions. But it is the internalization of these cultural differences which is reflected in the narrative and extends the concept of shame to the person of the author: "The novel interweaves its fantastic Pakistani narrative with an autobiographical account of the 'shame' of the writer-in-exile as he sets about making his novel."[5] Therefore, Rushdie's novel becomes a means for self-criticism, self-justification, and finally self-definition. His experiments with narrative voice mirror a need on his part to find his own voice.

Shame begins in the third-person narrative voice, in what appears to be an objective and distanced tone: "In the remote border town of Q.,

---

[4] Salman Rushdie, "Interview and Commentary: *Midnight's Children* and *Shame*," *Kunapipi* 7.1 (1985): 14.
[5] Michael Hollington, "Salman Rushdie's *Shame*," *Meanjin* 43 (1984): 406.

which when seen from the air resembles nothing so much as an ill-proportioned dumb-bell, there once lived three lovely, and loving, sisters."[6] The smooth course of the narration is soon interrupted by an aggressive voice which reminds the readers that what they are reading is a construct of the narrator's imagination. One level of narrative illusion is effectively destroyed and the narrator loses his transparence: "All this happened in the fourteenth century. I'm using the Hegiran calendar, naturally: don't imagine that stories of this type always take place longlong ago. Time cannot be homogenized as easily as milk, and in those parts, until quite recently, the thirteen-hundreds were still in full swing" (13). This second voice seems to represent the creator or the author.

In chapter two, the narration of the "story" itself is interrupted to insert information about the person of the author. The clear movement away from the simple mimetic representation which is inherent in this laying bare of the device of narration is balanced by an attempt to develop an intimacy between the reader and the author. The narrative voice in chapter two could be Rushdie's own. From this point in the narration the reader is confronted with two voices: one belonging to the omniscient and somewhat distanced narrator, and the other the voice of the intruding author. It should be noted, however, that there are instances in which the two voices merge. In other words, the narrative does not follow a strictly dialogical pattern, but rather demonstrates the disintegration of the voice of the omniscient narrator.

While expounding on the concept of shame as understood in the East, the narrator/author is drawn into explaining his personal sentiments on the subject. However, it is not shame on an historical level with which he has to struggle, but personal shame for being distanced from the culture he is describing:

> Outsider! Trespasser! You have no right to this subject . . . I know: nobody ever arrested me. Nor are they likely to. Poacher! Pirate! We reject your authority. We know you, with your foreign language wrapped around you like a flag: speaking about us in your forked tongue, what can you tell but lies? I reply with more questions: is history to be considered the property of the participants solely? In what courts are such claims staked, what boundary commissions map out territories? (28)

[6] Salman Rushdie, *Shame* (London: Jonathan Cape, 1983) 11.

This passage is an attempt on the part of the author to justify his views, as he does not feel himself to be fully a part of the world he has undertaken to depict, and seems to suspect the reader will not either. Yet he is not in a position to detach himself totally from it. The two intersecting voices could be seen as belonging to the narrator and his potential audience as well as representing the divisions within the authorial voice.

The next paragraph, in which the narrator/author confesses to being uncomfortably situated between two worlds, allows for a clearer demarcation between the two voices; on the one hand, there is the voice of the shame-ridden author and, on the other hand, that of the overseeing narrator: "I tell myself this will be a novel of leavetaking, my last words on the East from which, many years ago, I began to come loose. I do not always believe myself when I say this. It is part of the world to which, whether I like it or not, I am still joined, if only, by elastic bands" (28). In an interesting variation of the usual distancing of the narrative voice from the constructed world of the novel, Rushdie has presented his own authorial position as detached from the real world which is the subject of his mimetic efforts. At the same time, Rushdie has de-emphasized the illusion of the world of the novel while developing a confessional narrator who is more "real" than the world he describes.

A more primitive example of this narrative technique is present in Rushdie's first novel, *Grimus*. In this novel, the protagonist, Flapping Eagle, is an *American* Indian alienated from his native community. The extensive use of intertextuality and word play in *Grimus*, however, obscures the true import of the device and reduces it to a pun on the word "Indian." Yet the same dilemma is reflected in the split personality of the narrator of *Grimus*: "I was the boy. I was Joe-Sue, Axona Indian, orphan, named ambiguously at birth because my sex was uncertain until some time later, virgin, young brother of a wild female animal called Bird-Dog . . . It was my (his) twenty-first birthday, too, and I was about to become Flapping Eagle. And cease to be a few other people."[7]

The narrative voice of *Grimus* undergoes a series of transformations in relation to the fictional world of the novel. This is quite unlike the

---

[7] Salman Rushdie, *Grimus* (1975 rpt.; London: Granada, 1982) 15.

disquieting effect of the author's appearance in *Shame* in which he confesses to an alienation from the subject matter of his work. This does not mean that in *Shame* the distance between the author and the narrator has totally disappeared. In fact, it is not possible to label *Shame* an autobiographical novel in the traditional sense of the term. The plot itself is not strictly autobiographical. Yet an "autobiographical pact," as defined by Philippe Lejeune, exists in the novel. More explicitly than in *Midnight's Children* (Rushdie's second novel), the reader is invited to equate the narrative "I" with Rushdie. This is a significant development in Rushdie's use of autobiography. He moves from implicit references to his own past in *Midnight's Children* to what could be called personal confessions in *Shame*. As Rushdie himself has pointed out, in his first novel he was not yet able to signal clearly the tensions between the narrator and the author:

> . . . it's not surprising that people should assume that an autobiography is intended. However, I found, especially as he [the protagonist of *Midnight's Children*] grew older, that he and I diverged at many points strongly . . . I could not inform the reader that there are moments when the author and his narrator disagree. And I had to accept that that was, if you like, the price one had to pay for everything that he gave me. ("Interview and Commentary" 13)

In *Shame*, however, Rushdie allows direct confrontation between the author and the narrator to take place in the course of the narration. The author does not permit the narrator to dictate the narrative: the narrator is interrupted, and the narration resumes only when the author has completed his own confession. This change in narrative style, the roots of which are present in Rushdie's two earlier works, is to be understood as a means of personal catharsis for the author. The novel, then, is for Rushdie the process through which he comes to recognize his personal shame.

While detaching himself from the fictional world which condones "shame," Rushdie is forced to admit that this concept is an integral part of this own nature. In chapter seven, while relating an incident in London in which a Pakistani woman is murdered by her father for having brought dishonour upon the family, Rushdie finds himself in sympathy with the father:

> The story appalled me when I heard it, appalled me in a fairly obvious way. I had recently become a father myself and was therefore newly capable of estimating how colossal a force would be required to make a man turn a knife against his own flesh and blood. But even more appalling was my realization that, like the interviewed friends etc., I, too, found myself understanding the killer. The news did not seem alien to me. (115)

It would seem that Rushdie's bonds with the East are not as tenuous as the readers are at first led to believe. In his interviews, as in his fiction, Rushdie places his Eastern literary heritage in the foreground of his discussions. With regard to his second novel, he points out:

> . . . I think that when [*Midnight's Children*] is discussed in the West, it seems to get discussed almost entirely in terms of a certain string of writers who always get hung around its neck like a kind of garland, which is you know, García Márquez, Günter Grass, Rabelais, Laurence Sterne, Cervantes, Gogol, etc. So I thought that instead of talking about all that I'd try and talk about its Eastern literary ancestors and the sense in which it derives out of an Indian tradition which, to my mind, is much more important in it than this aforesaid list. ("Interview and Commentary" 6–7)

Despite the clarity of vision with which Rushdie proclaims his artistic aims, there are shades of uncertainty in the fictional voices which represent him. Like his protagonist, Omar Khayyam Shakil, Rushdie would seem to remain "a creature of the edge" (21). Rushdie welcomes the lack of univocality in his fiction; in fact, the quarrelling voices of *Shame* facilitate the juxtaposition of two cultural spheres. This is the type of co-existence to which the narrator of *Shame* aspires: "I, too, am a translated man. I have been *borne across*. It is generally believed that something is always lost in translation; I cling to the notion—and use, in evidence, the success of Fitzgerald-Khayyam—that something can also be gained" (29). The breakdown of Rushdie's narrative voices is a necessary step towards transformations and redefinitions of himself: "The translation of Rushdie may also be this uprooting from the East and this process of having to carry across material from another culture . . . Rushdie evokes the ambiguity which the Italian language shows so well, with its resemblance between *traduttore*, 'translator,' *traditore*, 'traitor.'"[8] For Rushdie, the internal divisions are indeed useful reminders of a complex and multifaceted personality.

Unlike Rushdie, the Iranian writer Sadegh Hedayat seems to have been less successful in resolving the dilemmas which his cross-cultural experiences wrought. Western critics often cite Hedayat's upbringing and education in the French system as the source of the disenchantments that led to his suicide. In a review of the French translation of Hedayat's novel, Gilbert Lazard postulates: "Fût-il un de ces Orientaux désaxés, captifs d'un Occident qui les laisse dans l'incertitude de leur destin?"[9] But there is little evidence in Hedayat's biography to support Lazard's assumptions.

Although at an early age Hedayat developed an interest in French culture, when he had the opportunity to continue his studies in France he chose to return to Iran. His appreciation of French did not go beyond the writing of a few short stories in French; he was far more interested in experimenting with forms of Persian prose. Predictably, however, European critics give little credence to Hedayat's role in forging a new style of Persian prose. There is an obvious contrast between Lazard's analysis and the following statement by one of Hedayat's own contemporaries, Bozorg Alavi:

> Die größte Bedeutung Hedajats liegt, außer in der künstlerischen Form seiner Kurzgeschichten, in seiner Sprache. Sicher hat kein iranischer Schriftsteller auf die Entwicklung der persischen Schriftsprache in so kurzer Zeit einen so starken und vielseitigen Einfluß ausgeübt wie er.[10]

The source of Hedayat's malaise is not to be found in his interest in Europe but rather in his desire to free his own art, and by extension Persian art, from the type of dependency which he believed first the Arab invasion and later European imperialism had imposed upon it. In the introduction to his edition of *The Rubayyiat of Omar Khayyam*, Hedayat

---

[8] Jean-Pierre Durix, "The Artistic Journey in Salman Rushdie's *Shame*," *World Literature Written in English* 23 (1984): 459.
[9] Gilbert Lazard, "Sadegh Hedayat, précurseur du nouveau réalisme iranien," *Le Figaro Littéraire* February 1954: 2.
[10] Bozorg Alavi, *Geschichte und Entwicklung der modernen persischen Literatur* (Berlin: Akademie, 1964) 168.

uses Khayyam's example to vent his disapproval of foreign influence in Persian art:

> Khayyam is the representative of the suffocated talent, tormented soul, the interpreter of the laments and the revolt of a great dignified, prosperous, and ancient Iran which little by little was being poisoned under the oppression of harsh Semitic thoughts and Arab domination.[11]

Veiled in these remarks is Hedayat's personal attack upon the contemporary monarch's (Reza Shah) naïve acceptance of Western norms. To counteract the effects of "Westomania," Hedayat advocated a return to Iran's own linguistic, cultural, and artistic heritage. In his texts, for instance, he insisted upon using Persian words where European equivalents had become customary.[12] The ultimate expression of Hedayat's preoccupation with the regeneration of Persian art is his only novel, *The Blind Owl*.

The narrator of *The Blind Owl* (he describes himself as a decorator of covers of pen-cases) claims to have suffered from a spiritual malady which has forever severed his ties with the outside world: "In the course of my life I have discovered that a fearful abyss lies between me and the other people and have realized that my best course is to remain silent and keep my thoughts to myself as long as I can."[13] However, the greatest threat posed to his already shattered personality issues from the depths of his subconscious: "My reflection had become stronger than my real self and I had become like an image in the mirror. I felt that I could not remain alone in the same room with my reflection. I was afraid that if I tried to run away he would come after me" (92). In this encounter with his *Doppelgänger*, the narrator's only source of solace is his art. Yet he fails to be inspired by what he considers to be the stultifying tradition of Persian art:

---

[11] Quoted in Hassan Kamshad's *Modern Persian Prose Literature* (Cambridge: University Press, 1966) 145.

[12] ". . . he would dig up words you couldn't find in dictionaries and then give them life! There were many such words. I remember, for example, him pointing out that people were always using the English word "net," as in "net profit," instead of the Persian *mok. Mok chand?*" from Donné Raffat's interview with Bozorg Alavi in *The Prison Papers of Bozorg Alavi: A Literary Odyssey* (Syracuse: Syracuse University Press, 1985) 63.

[13] D. P. Costello, trans., *The Blind Owl* (New York: Grove, 1969) 2.

> I used to work through the day, decorating the covers of pen-cases. Or, rather, I spent on my trade of pen-case decorator the time that I did not devote to wine and opium. I had chosen this ludicrous trade of pen-case decorator only in order to stupefy myself, in order somehow or other to kill time. (5)

In his repeated attempts to emulate the work of his predecessors, he merely clings to the techniques used in their art.

Like the Persian mystics, he fixes his artistic goals upon one abstract and predictably elusive object, "the ethereal girl." Although at first she is a source of inspiration to him, his obsession with her eventually becomes an obstacle to his creativity. He projects the divisions within himself onto the character of his beloved. When the ethereal girl is first introduced, her eyes are described as "frightening, magic eyes" at once attracting and terrifying the narrator. In the scene describing her final surrender, however, the dualism of her character becomes an obvious threat: "Was it possible that this woman, this girl or this angel of hell (for I did not know by what name to call her), was it possible that she should possess this double nature? She was so peaceful, so unconstrained" (20). Ultimately the narrator's attempts to revive his art through her bring forth disappointment and frustration. As he begins to confuse imagination and reality, his muse becomes indistinguishable from his wife, to whom he refers as "the bitch." The woman he finally murders could be either "the ethereal girl" or his wife.

While witnessing the dismembered corpse in his room he has the momentary illusion of having broken out of the repetitive patterns of his art; the beloved who is traditionally only an object of admiration is here physically and metaphorically destroyed. Yet even this act of self-assertion soon dissolves into despair:

> Within me I felt a new singular form of life. My being was somehow connected with that of all creatures that existed about me, with all the shadows that quivered around me . . . There was no conception, no notion which I felt to be foreign to me. I was capable of penetrating with ease the secrets of the painters of the past, the mysteries of abstruse philosophies, the ancient folly of ideas and species . . . it is at such times that the real artist is capable of producing a masterpiece. But I, listless and helpless as I was, I, the decorator of pen-case covers, what could I do? (22–3)

The narrator's inability to infuse life into his artistic heritage returns him once again to his threatening shadow, representing an empty shell of his "self." The attempts to make himself understood to his shadow result in a total negation of that self. In this sense, the narrator becomes "the blind owl," a mere reflection of others, forbidden both sight and insight in the symbolic darkness of his soul:

> My shadow had become more real than myself. The old odds-and-ends man, the butcher, nanny, the bitch and my wife, were shadows of me, shadows in the midst of which I was imprisoned. I had become like a screech-owl, but my cries caught in my throat and I spat them out in the form of clots of blood . . . My shadow on the wall had become exactly like an owl and, leaning forward, read intently every word I wrote. (123)

Although the narrator's despair and eventual madness can be analyzed on a psychoanalytical level,[14] a thematic analysis reveals that a preoccupation with art forms is the primary motivation of Hedayat's novel. The narrator rejects traditional Persian art without turning to other sources of inspiration. The image of the owl evoked throughout the novel further reinforces the theme of the failed quest for new means of artistic expression; in the tradition of Persian mysticism, the owl is the only creature which refuses to embark on the search for the Divine.[15] The novel's ending on a sinister note reflects Hedayat's own disgust with the rigidity of traditional Persian literature, which does not allow for innovation, and with the mere mimicking of Western models. Whether Hedayat's suicide is to be seen as a direct consequence of this position will remain open to speculation. What is certain, however, is Hedayat's obsession with finding an appropriate voice from within which would have the strength to withstand cultural confrontations.

Tayeb Salih's *Season of Migration to the North* actualizes the clash of cultures implicit in Hedayat's novel. The protagonist of Tayeb Salih's novel, Mustapha Sa'eed, suffers more intensely from cultural displacement. For him, there are no easy escapes from a double vision acquired

---

[14] See Carter Bryant's "Hedayat's Psychoanalysis of a Nation," in *Hedayat's* The Blind Owl: *Forty Years After*, ed. Michael C. Hillmann, Middle East Monographs, 4 (Austin: Universty of Texas Press, 1978) 153–67.
[15] Mohammad R. Ghanoonparvar, *"Buf-e Kur* as a Title," in *Hedayat's* The Blind Owl: *Forty Years After* 69.

through a long apprenticeship in colonial schools and in England. Although after his return to the Sudan Mustapha Sa'eed tries to become reintegrated in the life of his village, he cannot break with his past experience in the West. His sudden disappearance from the village, after relating part of his life story to the narrator, is indicative of a failure to reconcile the divisions within his character.

The narrator's identification with Mustapha Sa'eed further enhances the impression of the split personality of the protagonist. In many respects, the narrator and Mustapha Sa'eed are indistinguishable from one another. Aside from similarities in their education in the West, their shared vision allows them to be seen almost as one character. On the level of the narrative, Mustapha Sa'eed's own reminiscences are embedded in the frame story related by the narrator. In many instances the voice of the narrator is replaced by Mustapha Sa'eed's. As a result, the narrator's first-person account and Mustapha Sa'eed's become interwoven. Moreover, in the course of the narration, the narrator even begins to merge with the protagonist:

> Was it likely that what happened to Mustapha Sa'eed could have happened to me? He had said that he was a lie, so was I also a lie? I am from here—is not this reality enough? I too had lived with them. But I lived with them superficially, neither loving nor hating them.[16]

Yet, the two characters never completely merge. On the contrary, towards the end of the novel, the narrator perceives Mustapha Sa'eed as his rival. When he enters Sa'eed's study he is haunted by an already fading image of his opponent:

> I struck a match. The light exploded on my eyes and out of the darkness there emerged a frowning face with pursed lips that I knew but could not place. I moved towards it with hate in my heart. It was my adversary Mustapha Sa'eed. The face grew a neck, the neck two shoulders and a chest, then a trunk and two legs, and I found myself standing face to face with myself. This is not Mustapha Sa'eed—it's a picture of me frowning at my face from a mirror. (135)

This passage, along with the juxtaposed voices of the narrator and

---

[16] Denys Johnson-Davies, trans. *Seasons of Migration to the North* (1969; rpt. Washington D.C.: Three Continents, 1985) 49.

Mustapha Sa'eed, would seem to allow a Freudian interpretation. Many critics have explored the possibility of such readings.[17] But, to regard Mustapha Sa'eed merely as the narrator's subconscious would not give enough weight to the ending of the novel. Secondly, as Mohammad Shaheen has argued, there are unresolved ambiguities which undermine a simple equation of the two characters: ". . we do not know whether the narrator is struggling for or against Mustapha Sa'eed."[18] Other differences are to be inferred from the narrator's depiction of Mustapha Sa'eed.

The image of the young Sa'eed which emerges from the fragments pasted together by the narrator is that of a man lured towards the West, with the hope of casting himself in a new mould: "The whole of the journey I savoured that feeling of being nowhere, alone, before and behind me either eternity or nothingness . . . Here, too, was a desert laid out in blue-green, calling me, calling me" (27). The deliberate distance with which Mustapha Sa'eed approaches the outside world allows him the freedom of the wanderer. At the same time, it deprives him of a sense of belonging. After his arrival in England, he shows clear signs of alienation. His mastery of English, which had singled him out among his countrymen, proves to be inadequate: "My mind was like a keen knife. But the language is not my language; I had learnt to be eloquent in it through perseverance" (29). Moreover, he believes his initiation into Western culture to be tainted with artificiality: "From [Mrs. Robinson] I learnt to love Bach's music, Keat's poetry, and from her I heard for the first time of Mark Twain. And yet I enjoyed nothing" (28). To overcome his alienation, he willingly adopts the role of the outsider, confident of his ability to impose himself as an intruder. On the one hand, he sees himself through the eyes of the women who reduce him to stereotypes of "the African": "There came a moment when I felt I had transformed in her eyes into a naked, primitive creature, a spear in one hand and arrows in the other, hunting elephants and lions in the jungles. This was fine" (38). On the other hand, he hopes to use this role-playing in order to subdue his lovers: "Yes, my dear sirs, I came as an intruder,

---

[17] See Roger Allen's analysis and his references to other sources in *The Arabic Novel: An Historical and Critical Introduction* (Syracuse: Syracuse University Press, 1982).

[18] Mohammad Shaheen, "Tayeb Salih and Conrad," *Comparative Literature Studies* 22 (1985): 163.

into your very homes: a drop of the poison which you have injected into the veins of history. I am no Othello. Othello was a lie" (95). Predictably, he becomes the victim of his own mask. Having resolved to be the dominator, he becomes the dominated; when Jean Morris coerces him into carrying out her suicide, Mustapha Sa'eed has lost control of his own fate:

> Slowly I raised the dagger and she followed the blade with her eyes; the pupils widened suddenly and her face shone with a fleeting light like a flash of lightning. She continued to look at the blade-edge with a mixture of astonishment, fear, and lust. Then she took hold of the dagger and kissed it fervently. Suddenly she closed her eyes and stretched out in the bed, raising her middle slightly, opening her thighs wider. "Please, my sweet," she said, moaning: "come- I'm ready now." When I did not answer her appeal she gave a more agonizing moan. She waited. She wept. Her voice was so faint it could hardly be heard. "Please darling." (164)

This logic of the subjugation of the subjugator, as we saw in the preceding chapter, has been well elucidated by Malek Alloula. In the preoccupation of the French photographer with erotic representations of Algerian women, Alloula sees a testimony of the photographer's and, by extension, the colonizer's "obsessive neurosis" (122) and ultimate impotence. He argues that the exaggerated and false portraits of Algerian women and society are replacements for what is denied to the gaze of the photographer. By the same token, Mustapha Sa'eed's adoption of the role of intruder and his murder of Jean Morris are expressions of his powerlessness vis-à-vis the West. His withdrawal to a secluded village in the Sudan is an extension of this defeat and a last effort to separate himself from that world which threw him into uncertainty about himself. This desire to disentangle the self and the other is reflected in his carefully hidden "English" library. The incongruous presence of this room in the midst of a desert hut shocks the narrator: "How ridiculous! A fireplace—imagine it! A real English fireplace with all the bits and pieces . . . on either side of the fireplace were two victorian chairs covered in a figured silk material, while between them stood a round table with books and notebooks on it" (136). This room is also a symbol for the attraction which persists in the hidden recesses of Mustapha Sa'eed's mind. In a letter written shortly before his disappearance, he confesses to the narrator: ". . . mysterious things in my soul and in my blood impel me towards faraway parts that loom up before me and cannot be ignored" (67).

The dedication of his unfinished autobiography is another revealing testimony to Sa'eed's incurable duality of character: "To those who see with one eye, speak with one tongue and see things as either black or white, either Eastern or Western" (150–51). The blank pages of the autobiography are themselves startling confessions of a restless wanderer. In this sense, Mustapha Sa'eed's life is a never-ending "season of migration" to regions beyond his grasp.

If the ending of the novel, with the narrator staying afloat "half-way between north and south" (167), is an indication of the resolution of the dilemma of the divided self, then the narrator, unlike Mustapha Sa'eed, has adopted a position of mediation. However, the same cathartic act of retelling and reconstructing does not release the protagonist from his inner turmoils. On a larger scale, the dilemma still persists. Tayeb Salih's own reflections on East-West encounters bring him closer to the position adopted by Sadegh Hedayat: ". . . the interaction between the Arab Islamic world and Western European civilization is determined by illusions which exist on both sides."[19] In his fictional representation Tayeb Salih demonstrates a similar conviction; Mustapha Sa'eed is a victim not only of Western misperceptions but also of his own equally flawed perception of the West.

The issues which plague cross-cultural travellers from the East are presented in the foregoing works as complex problems, with both internal and external roots, not easily overcome through tidy poetic resolutions. It is, in fact, the very absence of smooth transitions from East to West which sparks the creation of such works and determines their tone. The voice which these writers adopt reflects their personal tribulations. Yet this same discordant voice and its stubborn refusal to merge with that of the "other" allows the unique position of the Eastern writer to be heard.

---

[19] Quoted in Shaheen 162.

Chapter Four

Writing in the Step-Mother Tongue

> Pour profaner le sanctuaire somptueux d'une langue, il faut y déposer une partie de soi—offrande mémorable et tatouée, ce livre! C'est pourquoi, je demeure ici entre les mains de la langue française. Langue que j'aime—je le répète—comme une belle et maléfique étrangère.[1]
>
> (Abdelkebir Khatibi)

Most writers whose works have been examined thus far have overcome Mustapha Sa'eed's dilemma of the blank page in so far as they do not aspire to the model of ". . . those who see with one eye, speak with one tongue and see things as . . . either Eastern or Western" (150–51). Yet even those Eastern writers who approach a second language with apparent ease are given to reflection upon their choice of an alien language. They, too, are keenly aware of having adopted what Bharati Mukherjee has called, the "step-mother tongue."[2]

As defined by Mukherjee, this term applies only to those writers who use a second language without attempting to "mimic perfectly the colonial [language]" (147), thereby resisting the literary traditions of the second language through subversion and reinvention. Set against this group, Mukherjee envisions another group of complacently "colonized" or "Orientalized" writers. In actuality, however, the delineations are not marked with the precision demanded by Mukherjee; the very act of mimicking suggests a degree of self-consciousness. Perhaps a clearer demarcation is to be made between the writers who articulate and display

---

[1] *La Mémoire tatouée* (Paris: Denoël, 1971) 13.
[2] "Mimicry and Reinvention," in *The Proceedings of the Triennial Conference of CACLALS*, Part Two, ed. Uma Parameswaran (Calcutta: Writers Workshop, 1983) 147.

through their medium the fear of being mere "displacements in the discourse of the other,"[3] and those who believe they are able to impose themselves upon a second language by blending in. In either case the balance between the self and the other is extremely precarious. When the rights of the mother tongue of an author are usurped, writing itself becomes an act of compromise between two contending cultural spheres. Ultimately one can only speak of degrees of compromise.

One situation in which an author is made more acutely aware of his or her choice of the medium of expression is that of exile. For some, the barrier between a native language and that of their adopted homeland proves to be insurmountable; in such instances, the questions of identity and language are inextricably linked. For example, the Iranian writer Mahshid Amir-Shahy sees her exile in Paris as an impediment to her creativity:

> I long to speak our mother tongue, whose alleyways and twistings are my second nature, whose delicacies I feel, in whose thoughts I appreciate the characteristic gleam. It's a language whose words I can piece together and set in place like jewels in their setting. I can mold its pliant syllables like wax and give it new possibilities; I can use it to bargain in the marketplace, to bicker with my sister, to give my daughter lessons and to write my stories. Now and again, after an interval of days, or of hours, I hear once more behind the door of some avenue in Paris the warmth of the Persian tongue ... and moment by moment the sorrow of exile approaches the limits of madness.[4]

Shortly after the publication of this statement, Amir-Shahy returned to Iran in an obvious attempt to become reintegrated in her own linguistic and cultural milieu. Her flight from exile stands as proof that repatriation through language is not always possible or desirable. On yet another level, Amir-Shahy's return to Iran implies that she perceived her efforts to preserve Persian language and literature in exile as futile; in Paris she would always risk being isolated from the currents of her own literature.

The same concerns which brought about Amir-Shahy's journey homeward are explored in Naïm Kattan's short story, "Le Gardien de

---

[3] *After the Last Sky* 140.
[4] Quoted in Michael Beard and Hasan Javady's "Iranian Writers Abroad: Survey and Elegy," *World Literature Today* 60.2: 258.

l'alphabet." Ali Souleyman's conviction that the sacred Koranic alphabet of the Turkish language must not be replaced by a Latin script makes him an outcast in his own society. This alienation becomes even more pronounced in Arab countries where his accent in Arabic receives more attention than his ambitious project. This sense of exile becomes permanent with his decision to settle down in a seemingly remote city in Canada: "C'est au cours de cette longue conversation que le pope lui parla d'une ville lointaine, perdue dans les neiges de l'Amérique et où les fidèles avaient construit une mosquée: Edmonton."[5]

In Edmonton, once again, Ali finds his compatriots and co-religionists uninterested in reinstating the old alphabet. Faced with this final rejection, he embarks on the gargantuan task of rewriting Turkish texts in Arabic script. However, the preservation of the texts soon becomes an end in itself: "Ali lisait rarement les ouvrages qu'il conservait" (117). Ironically, while he obsessively copies texts, he becomes increasingly less interested in the larger cultural sphere from which they emerge. His aims are so obscured that he neglects to teach Turkish to his own children, although he had originally intended to preserve the old alphabet for the younger generation of Turks. Even when the validity of his ambitions is questioned by the visiting Turkish philologue, Behjet Hamid, whom he has long admired, Ali prefers to turn a blind eye to the fact that he has deliberately placed himself in a cultural vacuum: "Mais c'est un fait, mon cher ami, c'est de l'histoire. Nous vivons le présent" (124). For Ali it is the role rather than the task which has gained significance. Accordingly, he shows no interest in his daughter's eagerness to join him in his efforts. He had hoped to pass on the role of "gardien de l'alphabet" to one of his sons: "Dommage qu'Amina soit une fille" (125). This very conclusion suggests that during the long period of collecting, cataloguing, and copying texts Ali has gradually, and perhaps subconsciously, realized that his language cannot be safeguarded against change. His lack of interest in the substance of his library would seem to be a direct consequence of his tacit understanding that the essence of all language is persistently elusive.

---

[5] Naïm Kattan, "Le Gardien de l'alphabet," in *La Traversée* (Montreal: Hurtubise, 1976) 112.

In his position as a multicultural writer, Naïm Kattan has himself been confronted with problematic juxtapositions of languages. He maintains an attachment to Arabic, which he regards as his mother tongue, and believes that in his writing there are remnants of what he himself labels "le discours arabe." Yet in his description of what constitutes the essence of Arabic writing he fails to put this essence in concrete terms: "Dans le discours arabe, il y a beaucoup de mots, les gens parlent beaucoup mais l'essentiel est très peu dit. Mais il est exprimé quand même" (Allard 15). Furthermore, he confesses that French has obscured some of the ways in which Arabic used to influence his writing. In an interesting example Kattan describes his difficulty in recognizing his own work in an Arabic translation:

> Il y a deux ans, il y a un Musulman, en Israël, qui a lu *Adieu Babylone* et a décidé d'en traduire un chapitre en arabe. Il l'a fait et me l'a envoyé après. Et j'ai lu *Adieu Babylone* qui se passe dans un pays arabe traduit en arabe. Ç'a [sic] été une expérience dure et très étrange. Dure tout de même parce que je ne m'y suis pas reconnu, écrit dans ma langue maternelle. Je lisais ce chapitre que j'ai écrit moi-même et je ne me reconnaissais pas. Je me suis donc dit: Mon Adieu n'est pas simplement las fin d'une histoire mais aussi le début d'une autre vie. (Allard 16)

The new beginning to which Kattan refers has not consisted of a simple integration into French language and culture. In this realm, also, Kattan has cautiously opted for distance. Instead of living in France, he has chosen Quebec with the express intention of being "vraiment dans un rapport d'échange (critique) avec la mère-culture française" (Allard 9).

For his part, Kattan appears to be content with the subtle presence of a multi-layered linguistic and literary heritage in his writing. His many cross-cultural encounters have taught him that more than one language or literary tradition will shape his texts. Kattan's acceptance of the continuous confrontation of languages in fact enables him to be at once within and outside any linguistic system.

The Moroccan writer and critic, Abdelkebir Khatibi, like Kattan does not envision undisturbed juxtapositions of languages. In his study of bilingual writing in North African literature and his autobiographical work, *La Mémoire tatouée*, Khatibi describes the bilingual writer's relationship to a second language in terms of a constant dualism of love and hate. His pronouncements, in *Maghreb pluriel*, on Maghrebian writing in French can be extended to other categories of multi-lingual or multi-cultural literature:

> ... la langue étrangère, dès lors qu'elle est interiorisée comme écriture effective, comme parole en acte, transforme la langue première, elle la structure et la déporte vers l'intraduisible. J'avancerai ceci: la langue dite étrangère ne vient pas s'ajouter à l'autre, ni opérer avec elle une pure juxtaposition: chacune *fait signe* à l'autre, l'appelle à se maintenir comme dehors. Dehors contre dehors, cette étrangeté: ce que désire une langue ... c'est d'être singulière, irréductible, rigoureusement autre. (186)

Khatibi also foresees the mutual interferences of two languages as a positive step towards a synthesis—"un récit qui parle en langues" (186). That is to say, a literature which transcends the limits of specific languages and which does not resist translation.

In practice, polyglot writers have experienced more the tensions described by Khatibi and less the linguistic reconciliation. For instance, the Turkish writer, Saliha Scheinhardt, whose works in German address the problems of Turkish immigrants in Germany, sees herself at once lured to and repelled by a language which remains stubbornly alien:

> Ich schreibe in Deutsch. Es ist ungemein schwer—so reizvoll es auch ist, in einer Fremdsprache zu experimentieren—das Leben eines bestimmten Kulturkreises und Sprachraumes in einer anderen Sprache in literarischer Form wiederzugeben. Hinzu kommt, daß Deutsch immer noch eine Fremdsprache für mich ist.[6]

The medium chosen by Scheinhardt is particularly suitable to the thematic focus of her works, namely the voluntary exile of her compatriots: "Dieses Buch kann nur ein bescheidener Beitrag sein. Ein Beitrag zum Verständnis, warum Menschen ihre Heimat verlassen müssen, wie sie das Leben im selbstgewählten Exil meistern" (8). Writing in a second language might distance her from the subject of her studies. Yet this same technique threatens to implicate her in the fate of the characters in her works.[7]

---

[6] Saliha Scheinhardt, "Introduction" to *Und die Frauen weinten Blut* (Berlin: Express, 1980) 9.

[7] In an article in the February 9, 1986 issue of *The German Tribune* Scheinhardt is quoted

The same path has been trodden by authors who, because of a colonial experience, have had a second language imposed on them. Numerous "Indo-Anglian" and African writers have had to tackle the thorny issue of the bridge between language and identity. As demonstrated in the example of the Tamil poet R. Parthasarathy, bilingual writers rarely attain a state of perfect linguistic harmony:

> My situation in the context of Indian verse in English can be described as fluid. Today, I find myself in a situation of bilingualism, of being at home in two languages, English and Tamil. And this bilingualism has set up a painful, but nevertheless fruitful, tension with regard to poetry.[8]

Other writers from former British or French colonies, in Bharati Mukherjee's classification the "reinventors," insist upon conveying the spirit of their own language and culture through the medium of a Western language. It is to this end that they submit their step-mother tongues to drastic transformations.

As argued by Mukherjee, the changes imposed on European languages can prove to be the non-native writers' only means of self-assertion. By distorting the language of the other, bilingual writers can awaken their readers to the importance of another culture hidden behind a Western mode of expression. Nonetheless, to return to Khatibi's remarks in *La Mémoire tatouée*, there is always the danger of losing too much of oneself in the process of manipulating the discourse of the other.

In the introduction to her novel, *Javady Alley*, the Iranian writer Manny Shirazi points out: "I would have liked to have written my first book in Farsi, but as I was unable to I wrote it in English."[9] Without further elucidating the reasons which compel her to write in English, Shirazi goes on to confess, with an obvious bitterness, that the completion of the book was contingent upon her learning "Queen's English." It appears that, for Shirazi, writing in English is equated with a full-fledged linguistic and cultural deracination. At least in the introduction, she demonstrates a reluctance to disturb the "correctness" of

---

as having said that she perceives of certain similarities between herself and the characters of her stories.
[8] R. Parthasarathy, "Whoring after English Gods," in *Writers in East-West Encounter: New Cultural Bearings*, ed. Guy Amirthanayagam (London: Macmillan, 1982) 71.
[9] Manny Shirazi, *Javady Alley* (London: Women's Press, 1984).

English. To be understood by British and North American audiences, Shirazi seems to be saying, she must learn to speak "their" language.

This conviction is manifest in her painstaking attempts to render into English the cultural setting of the novel. To bridge the gap between herself and her readers, Shirazi provides a glossary of Persian words, accompanied by a list of relevant historical events, but now and then she abandons her zeal for translation and introduces untranslated and untranslatable text. In one instance, a children's game, *alac do lac*, is only transliterated (17); no further explanation is provided in the glossary or in the context. One wonders, if while writing of childhood reminiscences, Shirazi has set aside her linguistic self-consciousness. In contrast to this example, many passages of the novel appear to have been concocted by a meticulous translator:

> I ate the bread and the cheese and sweet tea; it wasn't really so bad. Granny always said, "cheese is good for you." But I would have liked it if we had had chips, preferably with eggs and tomatoes. (19)

Although the word "chips" is a literal and correct translation from Persian into British English, it fails to bring about the desired effect; the English reader will be puzzled by the description of the meal, while the Iranian reader will recognize a discordant note. Despite the attempt to channel the Persian character and setting of her novel into patterns of English, Shirazi is unable to produce a complete cultural transplant. Even when she is successful in finding the English equivalent, she is clearly uneasy with her choice. Repeatedly, she comes up against a linguistic layer which resists easy renditions in the idiom of the other. Hence, the occasional lines of Persian scattered throughout the text which are in apparent contradiction with the goal of translating the entirety of her text into "Queen's English." These textual incongruities stand out as involuntary acts of self-defiance.

Manny Shirazi's use of English is an example of cautious initiation into a new language. Her work mirrors the hesitations and tensions inherent in any crossing of cultural boundaries; her self-consciousness indicates that although she is aware of being an outsider in the framework of the English language, she has not yet become confident in her "subversion" of that language. Therefore, she wavers between a desire to be understood by a broader audience and the need to speak in her own voice.

In *The Book of Absent People*, Taghi Modarressi shows himself eager to incorporate aspects of his own language in his writing. In fact, he deliberately juxtaposes English and Persian. As a result, the novel, his first in English, becomes an experiment in bilingual writing. Hence, one reviewer's comments: "These visions are prose poems. Modarressi writes like a poet in translation, with idiomatic grace and yet with a hint of grief about what is being lost or only stabbed at because the language is not Persian or at least Arabic."[10] Unlike Shirazi, Modarressi does not introduce Persian script in his text. Instead he uses direct translation: ". . . initially I did not write to publish in English . . . when I translated the novel from Farsi to English, I tried to do it in a concrete transliteral fashion. It would have been impossible to transplant the atmosphere of the novel into an English language form."[11]

Although thematically Modarressi's work remains within the limits of the genre of the novel of social concern (the story revolves around mysterious disappearances of characters, political imprisonments, and street riots), in its linguistic expression it resists all conventions. If the prefatory reference to Attar's *The Conference of the Birds* is intended to sum up the poetic essence of the novel, *The Book of Absent People* must be interpreted as an invitation to a linguistic odyssey:

> Oh, may your journey to the border of Sheba be happy.
> May *your speaking the language of the birds* with Solomon be happy.
> Hold back the demon in chains and in prison
> So you will be the keeper of the secret like Solomon.[12]
> [My emphasis]

The narrator of Modarressi's novel may not speak "the language of the birds," but he is successful in constantly thwarting the reader's linguistic

---

[10] Christiana Robb, "Review of The Book of Absent People," *The Boston Globe* 7 March 1986: 12. Robb's unfamiliarity with the cultural background of Modarressi's novel is immediately apparent in the segment of the review quoted here: Arabic would not have played a part in Modarressi's decision to write in English. The assumption that Arabic is central to Iranians is a common misconception.
[11] From private correspondence.
[12] Taghi Modarressi, *The Book of Absent People* (New York: Doubleday, 1986).

"horizon of expectations." With ease, he moves from English to direct translations of Persian sayings, while no explanations or glossary definitions are provided to supplement the purely contextual knowledge of the audience. For example when we read, "You have to find your brother Zia among your own relatives, not among strangers. You must know your own family first, and then start attacking this one and that one's leg" (56), the significance of the speech is not obscured; it is understood that "attacking other people's legs" means making demands of others. Yet the sense of local colour reinforced by the narrator's idiolect postpones the uninitiated reader's identification with the world of the fiction. Because the reader is required to sift through the cryptic language of the text, the act of reading becomes a rite of passage into a new mode of speech—to coin a new phrase in the spirit of the novel, "Farso-Anglian." Modarressi himself adheres to the notion of "writing with an accent"[13] and demands that his readers experience it, if only indirectly.

An interesting counter-example to Modarressi's use of Persian expressions is that of Roy Mottahedeh in his semi-fictional *The Mantle of the Prophet*. To endow the narration of the life of Ali Hashemi with authenticity, Mottahedeh frequently introduces translations from Persian: "Eventually the crowd became so thick that, as one says in Persian, 'a dog wouldn't recognize its master.'"[14] The interjection, "as one says in Persian," is intended to redirect the reader's attention to the flow of the English text. Always careful to avoid a mental digression on the part of the reader, Mottahedeh provides the English equivalent of Persian idioms: "Parviz said, 'we're lending each other bread' (which is the Persian equivalent of 'you scratch my back and I'll scratch yours')" (47).

In contrast to Mottahedeh, Modarressi breaks down the mediative barrier between the two languages and directly presents "what one says in Persian" even when there is risk of incomprehension:

> Even now, after some thirty-odd years, they still talked about it as though it had happened yesterday. They had never given any thought to the children

---

[13] From private correspondence.
[14] Roy Mottahedeh, *The Mantle of the Prophet: Religion and Politics in Iran* (New York: Simon and Schuster, 1985) 16.

of Homayundokht, God forgive her soul, and used to melodramatically describe *the onion and the garlic of that story* in front of my Khan Brother Zia and my sister Iran as though those two were deaf and couldn't hear them. (15, my emphasis)

The general sense of the expression, "the onion and garlic of the story," can be surmised from the context; what is implied is an unnecessarily detailed and painful account of the character Homayundokht's death. Although the bilingual reader is more actively drawn into the description, he, too, will require some effort to switch from one linguistic/cultural sphere to another; the message appearing in the guise of English must still be decoded. While one group of readers might be baffled, another group must carry out simultaneous translations.

In other passages, a broader familiarity with Persian language and culture is taken for granted:

> Then I set off again in a hurry. From a hundred paces away, I heard his whistling begin once again. He was whistling the Chekavak Corner of the Scale of Homayun. When he reached the Bee-Dad Corner, he started twittering like a nightingale—a constant massaging twitter that polished the wet street. (13)

In this context, transliteration rather than translation is the only bridge between the narrative voice and the reader. The audience unfamiliar with Iranian music will only grasp a fleeting reference to music but will not be aware of the pun made on the name of Homayundokht and the musical scale called Homayun. Similarly, the feast of "the killing of Omar," a Shi'ite annual ritual in which effigies of the second Caliph are burned in a demonstration of hatred, is not elucidated:

> Early in the morning they went to the bathhouse together, and with henna they drew flowers and leaves on their foreheads and the backs of their hands. Early in the evening they dressed in their flashy red dresses. They sat in front of a mirror and, old as they were, they applied their make-up with seven brushes. As the guests arrived, the sisters poured pumpkin seeds and cantaloupe seeds into a pan and insisted that everyone put on a toothy grin so the seeds would burst open and smile like Damghan pistachios. Two hours into the evening, they set fire to the effigy of Omar, made of tissue paper and wearing a red costume, and they cried together with joy. (185)

The scene could be read as another example of local colour. In this type of reading, perhaps the associations with Homayundokht's suicide in flames will be discerned. However, the more significant relationship between a religious ritual celebrated in a domestic setting and the violence projected onto the streets of Tehran may be obscured. Underlying this description is the destructive force which later in the narrative takes hold of the entire country.

Another level of difficulty is posed by dialogues which amount to little more than direct rendering of speech from Persian. The following exchange between Rokni and his mother borders on the absurd, while the phrases are intended to convey the anguish and the frustration of both characters after the death of the patriarch of the family:

> "I want to open the doors of Homayundokht's room."
> "Rokni-jun, I beg of you, hold back and wait so we can think this through and learn what sort of dust we have to pour on our own heads. The sealed door is not easy to open."
> "I'll show you how easy it is." But when I examined the lock, I saw that to undo it was the work of an elephant. (165)

The repeated use of unfamiliar words and phrases still allows the reader a partial understanding. Yet it is clear that linguistic nuances will remain beyond some readers' grasp; "pouring dust on one's head" does not evoke the utter despair suffered by the characters. What Modarressi's narrative devices emphasize is the impossibility of bridging a cultural gap through language alone: "As far as the relationship between English and Farsi is concerned, I believe the dissimilarities override the similarities."[15] The underlying argument would seem to be that no glossary or network of authorial interjections can eliminate all possible readers' "spots of indeterminacy," especially in a work of bicultural or multicultural nature. In fact, as Reed Dasenbrock has argued, deliberate disorientation is often the essence of writing in a second language:

> Indeed, the meaningfulness of multicultural works is in large measure a function of their unintelligibility for part of their audience. Multicultural literature offers us above all an experience of multiculturalism, in which not everything is likely to be wholly understood by every reader. The texts

---

[15] From private correspondence.

often only mirror the misunderstandings and failures of unintelligibility in the multicultural situations they depict.[16]

Seen in this light, Modarressi's eccentric use of English alerts his readers to cultural norms beyond their grasp. He equates the act of reading with a symbolic quest into the realm of the unknown; in the reference to Attar's poem the reader is invited to "speak the language of the birds." But this journey to a new linguistic realm is, like the quest in *The Conference of the Birds*, never-ending. There exists an interesting analogy between the aimless wanderings of the protagonist, especially in the final scene of the novel, and the reader's sometimes unfruitful linguistic quest. At the end of the novel, like Rokni, the reader might shrug his shoulders in apparent incomprehension:

> Who knows? Maybe already they're wondering how I am and where I've gone. Am I alive, am I dead, what if I've been done away with, what if I, too, have joined the world of absent people? But now I think of other things. I loiter in the streets and stand in a line at the movie houses. If they stopped me and asked, "Rokni, what for?" I would shrug my shoulders. (206)

The note of indeterminacy on which the novel ends extends beyond the uncertainties of the fate of the protagonist/narrator; on another level, it reflects the author's first hesitant steps towards new creative acts and his concern with the reception of his novel in an English-speaking milieu. Yet this venture into the realm of multicultural writing indicates Modarressi's break from those writers in exile who continue to seek their audience in their native lands. In sharp contrast to Amir-Shahy, Modarressi has chosen immigration rather than exile and, as an immigrant writer, has launched on a path towards new means of expression.

Salman's Rushdie's *Grimus* is another example of experimental use of language. When published in 1975, the novel was at first favourably received only by science fiction readers and eventually became classified as a work of science fiction—this in spite of Rushdie's own statement: "I personally think it doesn't fit into any category . . . I don't think it's

---

[16] "Intelligibility and Meaningfulness in Multicultural Literature in English," *PMLA* 102 (1987): 12.

science fiction, anyway, because there's no science in it. It's a fantasy novel, really."[17] The debate concerning the genre of *Grimus* has not yet been settled;[18] the only point upon which Rushdie's critics agree is that both in form and composition *Grimus* is a hybrid. In it Rushdie brings together elements of Eastern and Western literatures and languages to create a literary puzzle.

The title itself initiates the game; it is an anagram of the name of the ancient Iranian mythical bird, Simurg. The reworking of myths and legends also extends to the plot of the novel which reads like a reversal of the storyline of a twelfth-century Persian allegorical poem, Farid ud-Din Attar's *The Conference of the Birds*—itself a rewriting of the myth of Simurg. As Rushdie's novel is largely based on Attar's poem, it may be useful to provide a brief summary of *The Conference of the Birds*.

In his allegorical work, Attar makes a pun on the name of the mythical bird Simurg: all birds of the universe set out on a quest for the essence of the Divine, which their guide reveals to be the bird Simurg living on the mountain of Kâf. Although the journey to the mountain is hazardous, a group of birds finally embarks on the search. At the end of their journey, when the thirty remaining birds reach their goal, they discover that through their quest for the Divine they themselves have become Simurg or incarnations of the Divine; in Persian *si murg* literally means "thirty birds":

> There in the Simorgh's radiant face they saw
> Themselves, the Simorgh of the world—with awe
> They gazed, and dared at last to comprehend
> They were the Simorgh and the journey's end.
> They see the Simorgh—at themselves they stare,
> And see a second Simorgh standing there
> They look at both and see the two are one.[19]

Rushdie signals his own re-arrangement of this myth by using the name

---

[17] "Interview," *Contemporary Authors*, 111 (1984): 415.
[18] See Uma Parameswaran's "Handcuffed to History: Salman Rushdie's Art," *Ariel* 14 (1983): 34–35 and Ib Johansen's "The Flight from the Enchanter: Reflections on Salman Rushdie's *Grimus*," *Kunapipi* 7.1 (1985): 20–32.
[19] Farid ud-Din Attar, *The Conference of the Birds*, trans. Afkham Darbandi and Dick Davis (Middlesex: Penguin, 1984) 219.

Simurg in the anagram title. Moreover, in the spirit of Attar's poem he leads his readers through a maze of details which make up the plot of the novel.

Four quotations serve as epigraphs to the novel: the first is from T. S. Eliot's *The Four Quartets*, the second from Fitzgerald's translation of Attar's *The Conference of the Birds*, the third from Ted Hughes; the fourth taken from I. Q. Gribb's "All-purpose Quotable Philosophy," is fictitious and belongs to the world of the novel itself. By juxtaposing allusions to both well-known literary texts and fictitious ones, Rushdie forces his readers to become active in deciphering what he presents in the guise of literary puzzles. Secondly, by quoting Fitzgerald, a literary figure with a reputation for altering original texts in his translations, Rushdie draws attention to the type of textual tampering which he himself is about to undertake in *Grimus*.

The second piece of the puzzle of "Grimus" is found in a rather cryptic passage in chapter ten which also foreshadows the outcome of the plot:

> The bird-kingdom is remarkably suitable for mythmakers... Consider too, the profusion of bird-Gods in Antiquity. The Phoenix. The Roc. The Homa... The Orosch. The Saëna. The Anqa. And of course, the master of them all, Simurg himself. (47–8)

In a subtle hint as to how to read the anagram of the title, Rushdie displays the word Simurg as well as its archaic and pre-Avestan form, Saëna. In the *Avesta* (the Zoroastrian Holy book), the word Saëna was translated as eagle or falcon.[20] The simultaneous reference to Simurg and Saëna at this early stage of the novel sets up an equation between the protagonist, Flapping Eagle, Saëna, Simurg, and Grimus, and hence reflects the final merging of Flapping Eagle and Grimus.

The significance of the title,[21] however, is not fully revealed until chapter fifty-four. In the previous chapter, the reader learns that Grimus is an anagram of Simurg; the allusion to Attar's mystical poem is then explained in what amounts to a summary of *The Conference of the Birds*:

---

[20] Mohammad Moïn, *Fahrang-e Moïn*, Vol. V (Tehran: Amir Kabir, 1967) 846.
[21] Although Rushdie refers specifically to the Myth of the Mountain of Kâf as it is used in *The Conference of the Birds*, he also evokes its use in other literary sources such as the *Shah Nameh*.

It's not his real name, Grimus. He told us so freely. He changed it from something unpronounceable when he arrived in this country some thirty years ago. True to himself, his adopted name is derived anagrammatically from a mythical bird: the Simurg . . . the Simurg, he told us eagerly, is the Great Bird. It is vast, all-powerful and singular. It is the sum of all other birds. There is a Sufi poem in which thirty birds set out to find the Simurg on the mountain where he lives. When they reach the peak, they find that they themselves are, or rather have become, the Simurg. The name, you see, means thirty birds. Fascinating. Fascinating. The myth of the Mountain of Kâf. (222–23)

All references to the myth of the mountain of Kâf are ultimately integrated into the plot of *Grimus* and the fate of its protagonist is revealed to be a palindrome—an inversion of the structure of *The Conference of the Birds*. Unlike the birds in Attar's poem, Flapping Eagle sets out on his journey to counteract the effects of a potion which has granted him eternal life. In the final scene of the novel, Flapping Eagle once again reverses the myth and resists an annihilation of his "self." Even after the personalities of Flapping Eagle and Grimus have merged, the former strives for a separate identity: "There is still an *I*. An *I* within me that is not *him*" (260). This is a far cry from the resigned reunion of the thirty birds of Attar's poem.

The process by which the reader arrives at an understanding of the overall structure of Rushdie's novel is similar to that followed in deciphering a puzzle. This very act of reading is thematized in a passage in chapter eight: Virgil Jones is seen busying himself with a jigsaw puzzle. While he attempts to explain the nature of Calf Island (Kâf) to Flapping Eagle, he accidentally scatters the pieces of the puzzle on the floor. As Flapping Eagle is frustrated in his efforts to put together the puzzle, and by extension to grasp the mysteries of Calf Island, Virgil Jones declares triumphantly: "That's my little joke . . . The jigsaw cannot be completed" (45). On one level, like the pun in Attar's poem, *Grimus* is Rushdie's "little joke" with the reader. The "Grimus" of the title becomes a grimace, or an aside, to the reader who has witnessed the unfolding of the plot only to discover that the plot itself is about the making of the anagram, *Grimus*.

Anagram and the correlated rearrangement of literary sources is, indeed, the motivating structural principle of *Grimus*. In chapter eighteen the device itself is laid bare; the passage in question concerns the creatures which inhabit one of the imaginary worlds of *Grimus*, "Gorfs," an anagram of "frogs": "The Gorfic planet is sometimes called Thera. It winds its way around the star Nus in the Yawy Klim galaxy of the Gorfic Nirveesu. This area is the major component of the zone sometimes termed the Gorfic Endimions" (68). A re-arrangement of this passage would read: "The Frogic planet is sometimes called Earth. It winds its way around the star Sun in the Milky Way galaxy of the Frogic Universe. This area is the major component of the zone sometimes termed the Frogic Dominions." While the reader is still struggling with the re-ordering of the letters of the previous passage, Rushdie directs his attention to the principle behind its composition and by extension to the principle behind the composition of his entire work:

> The Gorfic obsession with anagram-making ranges from simple re-arrangement of word-forms to the exalted level of the Divine Game of Order. The game extends far beyond mere letter-puzzling; the vast mental powers of the Gorfs make it possible for them anagrammatically to alter their very environment and indeed their own physical make up . . . The rules of the game are known as Anagrammar; and to hold the title of Magister Anagrammari is the highest desire of any living Gorf. (68)

Presented in this light, *Grimus* is an obsessive re-arrangement of word-forms and literary texts; it is an "anagrammatical" text whose structure is reminiscent of the multi-layered dimensions of Calf Island, which in Virgil Jones's description extends to all levels of reality: ". . . [you must concede] that an infinity of dimensions might exist, as *palimpsests*, upon and within and around our own, without our being in any wise able to perceive them" (55, my emphasis). This archetypal expression of the doctrine of "world and word as palimpsest," justifies Rushdie's linguistic, thematic, and structural transformation of other texts.

Yet, the success of Rushdie's literary collage relies upon wider knowledge of literature on the part of his readers. They must also recognize allusions to *The Poetic Edda*, *The Communist Manifesto*, *The Divine Comedy*, Shakespeare's texts, as well as Persian and Indian myths. Through his experiments with language, Rushdie thus requires his readers to reflect upon the larger context from which his work emerges.

In his later fiction, Rushdie has moved away from the degree of experimentation witnessed in *Grimus*, yet he has maintained an interest in asserting his own literary and cultural heritage. It is, therefore, not surprising that in her discussion of post-colonial Indian writing in English, "Mimcry and Reinvention," Bharati Mukherjee cites Rushdie's work as the most representative example of the new genre:

> Rushdie's work is primarily about establishing one's identity by indenting one's language on the ruins of the old. For him colonialism and English are bonus; this gives him two survival kits instead of one. His mimic-man character is a hollow man who wears a three-piece suit to hide a literal hole in his body, a hole out of which words drain out, one can also stuff the hole with new words. (155)

As the analysis of *Grimus* and *The Book of Absent People* reveals, both Modarressi and Rushdie have referred to Attar's *The Conference of the Birds*. This is not mere coincidence. The example both authors have followed is one in which many traditions have been brought together in a literary creation. As a mystic, Attar had already overstepped the boundaries of Muslim orthodoxy. In writing his allegorical poem he defied the norms anew by making use of a Zoroastrian legend. The end result, a mystic parable, was accordingly an expression of Attar's own aesthetic ambitions. Attar's boldness of vision is precisely what Rushdie, Modarressi, and writers like them hope to emulate. The linguistic experiments they carry out are a subtle response to Eurocentrism which simultaneously draws them closer to their step-mother tongue. The bridge of tongues these writers create can, therefore, bring about a type of poetic synthesis of East and West which is not yet reflected in reality.

Chapter Five
Satirical Treatments of the East-West Encounter

> Dead drunk, not like a common sot, one day
> Nasir-i-Khusraw went to take the air.
> Hard by a dung-heap he espied a grave
> And straightway cried, 'O ye who stand and stare,
> Behold the world! Behold its luxuries!
> Its dainties here—the fools who ate them here![1]
>
> (Nasir-i-Khusraw)

If the immediately foregoing authors have been preoccupied with ways of coming to terms with the West and their dual identity, there is another group of Eastern writers who not only question Western stereotypes of the East but also rather cynically refuse to believe that their eradication will lead to better mutual understanding. In its concern with cultural identification, this form of response, to be found in satirical treatments of East-West encounters, has much in common with the works examined in the previous chapters. There is, however, a difference in tone which distinguishes these representations from even the most introspective reflections on the East-West dichotomy we have seen so far.

Sadegh Hedayat's "The Caravan of Islam" satirizes religious fervour in Iran. It is presented in the form of the diary of an Arab journalist who accompanies a Muslim missionary delegation from Saudi Arabia to Europe. The form, diary, and the theme, religious conversion, of Hedayat's short story are reminiscent of the work of the earlier Iranian convert, Uruch Beg. It is not crucial to establish Hedayat's first-hand knowledge of *Don Juan of Persia*. What is important is Hedayat's particu-

---

[1] Blasphemous verses ascribed to Nasir-i-Khusraw, quoted in translation by Edward G. Browne in *A Literary History of Persia* Vol. II (Cambridge: University Press, 1956) 243.

lar use of the genre of the travelogue, which was one of the earliest forms of descriptions of the West. The satirical twists Hedayat gives the well-known conventions impugn, at least on one level, the authority of some of the most canonical Eastern sources on the West. Thematically, "The Caravan of Islam" also challenges the presumption that alien societies can be grasped through simple descriptions.

The first episode, which consists of an account of a meeting held before the departure of the mission, is intended as a mockery of the Muslim clergy's political ambitions. Divested of all political power in their native lands, the delegates set out to convert the infidels of Europe and to establish centers for "Islamic propaganda." Among their objectives is:

> To make the learning of Arabic obligatory. The infidels should acquire sufficient knowledge of Arabic to recite the Koran in suitable form. If they do not, however, grasp the meaning of what they recite, there should be no cause for alarm. In fact, it is preferable that they remain ignorant of the meaning.[2]

As shortly after their arrival in Berlin the treasurer absconds with the funds, the clergy are never given an opportunity to try out their plans. But their adventures in Europe shed new light on European attitudes towards the East.

While stranded in Berlin the delegates receive two offers of employment: one from the owner of a zoo and another from the director of a circus. Pressed by their financial needs the Muslims accept the first offer. In the zoo they are put on display and attract crowds of spectators. Like animals, they are reduced to mere objects to be photographed and talked about. Ironically, however, the Muslims are not offended by the treatment they receive and learn to profit from the European mania for exoticism; they are interviewed, photographed and perform prayers for a

---

[2] Sadegh Hedayat, "The Caravan of Islam" (Paris: Organisation des mouvements nationalistes des universitaires, chercheurs et intellectuels iraniens, 1982) 17. This text has not been translated into English. In fact, it has been largely ignored by Hedayat's critics. In his bibliography of Hedayat's works, *The Fiction of Sadegh Hedayat* (Lexington, Kentucky: Mazda, 1984), Iraj Bashiri makes no reference to it. This may be due to the critical nature and, to some, the offensive and sacrilegious language of Hedayat's short story. The translations are my own.

fee. Ultimately, they delude both the European observers and their compatriots, who mistake the appearance of the missionaries in numerous European newspapers for the success of their propaganda. This new wave of enthusiasm brings the delegates another form of financial success; more funds are sent from Muslim nations to expand what they believe to be a mission in Europe. This time the missionaries decide to invest the money in a tavern in Paris. It is in this location that the journalist finds the remaining delegates and interviews them for the last time.

In the final episode, the entire mission is revealed to have been carefully planned by the delegates as a means of deceiving Muslims and Europeans alike; as they raise their glasses to "the success of the caravan of Islam," the missionaries proudly confess that they had expected a favourable reception in Europe but that their victory had been beyond their expectations. But if the Muslim missionaries are shown as greedy and calculating manipulators, the manner of behaviour and the motivations of their Western observers are also questioned. One of the last questions the journalist asks concerns the reputation of Islam in Europe and the effect their conduct might have on European scholarly writings on Islam. In response, one of the former delegates points out: "all of that [European writing on Islam] is a vehicle for imperialism. These books are published to placate us and to better manipulate us" (40).

Hedayat's satire is directed towards the two opposing poles of Iranian society: those who believe in the benevolence of the West and others, weary of the West, who blindly place their trust in their own religion.[3] Because of mutual distrust between two cultures, moreover, Hedayat believes that East and West will always remain apart. He not only sees

---

[3] Hedayat made no secret of his hatred for religious, especially Muslim, influence in Iran. In chapter three, I have referred to his statement on the type of restrictions he believed Arab-Islamic influence to have placed on Iranian life. In his novel, *The Blind Owl*, we find passages such as: "A few days ago she brought me a prayer-book with half-an-inch of dust on it. I had no use, not only for prayer-books, but for any sort of literature that expressed the notions of the rabble. What need had I of their nonsense and lies? . . . As for mosques, the muezzin's call to prayer, the ceremonial washing of the body and rinsing of the mouth, not to mention the pious practice of bobbing up and down in honour of a high and mighty Being, the omnipotent Lord of all things, with whom it was impossible to have a chat except in the Arabic language—these things left me completely cold." (88)

the dialectic of the self and the other as the modus operandi of East-West relations but also predicts that it will always be the norm. As reflected in the words of one of the delegates, the synthesis of East and West, is in Hedayat's view not even desirable:

> Do you remember what Taj used to say of the philosophy of Islam, of Heaven and Hell? In the other world Muslim men would be given an angel who would have her feet in the East and her head in the West . . . I prefer to do hard labour and not be granted the angel whose head and tail cannot be collected in one place. (40)

The cynicism of these last lines is a far cry from Uruch Beg's final passionate confession. Though in very different tones, both statements underscore the difficulty of total "conversion," be it religious or cultural.

With less sarcasm, the Iranian satirist Iraj Pezeshkzad has also expressed doubt about the possibility of eliminating cultural prejudices in his extremely popular novel, *My Dear Uncle Napoleon*.[4] The novel is set during the Second World War and is a comic treatment of the popular Iranian belief that the British are always directly or indirectly involved in events which shape the history of their country. Ever since the Constitutional Revolution, during which the British lent support to the members of the Iranian clergy opposing the monarchy, Iranians have suspected the British of causing disruption in Iranian politics. As pointed out by Denis Wright in his study *The Persians Amongst the English*, this fear of the British has not subsided even after the revolution of 1979:

> I should have liked, had I felt competent to do so, to write a final chapter analysing the popular Persian view of the English. What lies behind the love-hate feelings towards us of so many Persians? . . . Why, even, today, so many Persians instinctively attribute much of what happens in their country to the English . . . Why do so many of them today believe that the Ayatollah Khomeini enjoys British support and that one only has, as they put it, to lift his beard to find "Made in England" printed underneath? (XVI)

Pezeshkzad capitalizes upon this national anxiety in his portrait of a retired serviceman who in his dotage, especially during the advance of

---

[4] Since its first publication in 1968, *My Dear Uncle Napoleon* has been reprinted eleven times; it was also adapted for a television series which rivaled the popularity of the novel.

the allied forces towards Iran, imagines himself a Napoleon-like figure. The title of Uncle Napoleon is bestowed upon him by relatives who, out of respect for his age and stature, humour his delusions of grandeur. In his long narrations inflicted upon family members, Napoleon gradually equates the skirmishes he had once witnessed in the South of Iran with the Napoleonic wars, and the tribal rebels become agents of the British Empire. In his increased paranoia, he begins to imagine that even those only remotely associated with the British, for instance his Indian neighbours, are spying on him. Uncle Napoleon's fear of the British so dominates his life that when he receives news that the allies are about to enter Tehran, he decides to flee the city:

> ... they will not wait. The British troops have mobilized towards Tehran. They may arrive any day now. Believe me I am not thinking of myself. I have always lived in danger and become accustomed to it. To quote Napoleon, "brave men are born of danger." I am merely concerned about my innocent children. I assure you the first thing the British will do in Tehran is to settle old accounts with me.[5]

By juxtaposing Uncle Napoleon's paranoid visions and the real threat, hardly perceived by the other characters, which the extended presence of the British posed to the political independence of Iran, Pezeshkzad demonstrates the extent to which myth and reality are intermingled in East-West relations. When an encounter between Uncle Napoleon and an Indian feigning to be an agent of the British[6] is orchestrated by relatives, the irony of the situation becomes clear; Uncle Napoleon is ridiculed by the same spectators who, years later, were to witness real confrontations between Iran and Britain. The *Inglis-ha*[7] Uncle Napoleon and his servant, Mash Ghasem, see in every "cross-eyed"[8] blond person

---

[5] Iraj Pezeshkzad, *My Dear Uncle Napoleon* (1968; rpt. London: Paka, n.d.) twelfth edition 175. The translations of this text are my own.

[6] Long after Uncle Napoleon's death, the narrator discovers that the same man was in reality an agent for the Germans.

[7] The plural of Englishman in Persian.

[8] Uncle Napoleon's servant is convinced that the dishonesty of the British has a clear manifestation in their physiognomy; he swears that every Englishman he has encountered is cross-eyed. In one episode he mistakes a man from the northern province of Gilan, unfortunate enough to have been both blond and cross-eyed, for an Englishman and attacks him in the market.

in the neighborhood were indeed cause for concern in the post-war history of Iran.

Underlying the comic tone in which Uncle Napoleon's negotiations are described is the general disbelief, also shared by the author, that Iran would ever be granted a status equal to that of Western powers. No doubt Pezeshkzad's own experiences as an Iranian diplomat[9] contributed to this skepticism. But even after the revolution, Pezeshkzad has maintained his cynicism. In the dedication to the twelfth edition of his novel, he joins his characters, Uncle Napoleon and Mash Ghasem, in a chorus:

> I always preferred Mash Ghasem to the other characters, for misfortune had distanced him from his beloved country of Ghiasabad. So allow me in memory of the eternal Mash Ghasem, Parviz Fannizadeh [the actor who played his role in the television series], to dedicate this book to all those who have been unwillingly separated from their own Ghiasabad, Iran.

The Iranian revolution, Pezeshkzad seems to imply, has redirected the age-old distrust of the British; the threat to Iran is no longer posed from foreign quarters but rather from within. He sees little difference between British imperialist ambitions in Iran and the present Iranian regime's policies which have internalized those same tendencies. In a collection of satirical essays published after the revolution, *International Brats*, Pezeshkzad is especially critical of those Iranians who fell prey to the rhetoric of revolution and accepted the new mask only to find themselves, shortly thereafter, in exile.[10] The title of one of these essays, "The Second Uncle Napoleon," is indicative of Pezeshkzad's continued pessimism; this second Uncle Napoleon is a parody of today's political elite in Iran.

A similar type of cynical self-criticism is found in Bapsi Sidhwa's satirical portrait of the Parsis of India in *The Crow Eaters*. Recognizing the self-reflexive dimensions of the title, a phrase which refers to those who talk too much, Sidhwa initially attempts to temper her satire:

> Because of a deep-rooted admiration for my community—and an enormous affection for its few eccentricities—this work of fiction has been a labour of

---

[9] The years in which *My Dear Uncle Napoleon* was composed, Pezeshkzad served as a diplomat in various Iranian embassies in Europe.

[10] Many of the essays in this volume are devoted to the former president of the Islamic Republic, Bani Sadr, and the leaders of various revolutionary groups who having been forced into exile have had to publicly deny their earlier support for the revolution.

love. The nature of satire being to exaggerate, the incidents of this book do not reflect at all upon the integrity of a community whose scrupulous honesty and sense of honour are renowned.[11]

Nevertheless, she proceeds to depict the political follies of her community in pre-independence India. By positioning themselves between the rulers, i.e. the British, and the native population of India, the Parsis become engaged in a dangerous political game originally intended to strengthen their position as a minority. These sentiments are echoed in the words of the protagonist, Faredoon Junglewalla:

> And where, if I may ask does the sun rise? No, not in the East. For us it rises—and sets—in the Englishman's arse. They are our sovereigns! Where do you think we'd be if we did not curry favour? Next to the nawabs, rajas and princelings, we are the great toadies of the British Empire! These are not ugly words, mind you. They are the sweet dictates of our delicious need to exist, to live and prosper in peace. Otherwise, where would we Parsis be? Cleaning out gutters with the untouchables—a dispersed pinch of snuff sneezed from the heterogeneous nostrils of India! Oh yes, in looking after our interests we have maintained our strength. (12)

Although this complacency bears fruit in so far as Faredoon and others who share his ambitions succeed in siding at once with the British, the Hindus, and Muslims, it backfires and makes the Parsis, at least psychologically, as dependent as the British on the logic of imperialism.

The contradictions do not become apparent until Faredoon and his family visit England. Prior to their departure Faredoon, his wife, Putli, and his mother-in law, Jerbanoo fantasize about the exotic land from which their rulers originate and eagerly await a first-hand experience:

> To them England was a land of crowns and thrones; of tall, splendidly attired, cool-eyed noblemen and imposing, fair-haired ladies gliding past in gleaming carriages; of elegant lords in tall hats and tails, strolling with languid ladies who swept spotless waterfront promenades with trailing gowns, their gestures gracious and charming, marked by an exquisite reserve. (252)

Soon after their arrival in England, however, the group is disillusioned with the realities of England; they see the imperfections which they

---

[11] Bapsi Sidhwa, *The Crow Eaters* (New York: St. Martin's, 1984), Author's Note.

themselves had consented to overlook in India: "Where were the kings and queens, the lords and women with haughty, compelling eyes and arrogant mien? They realised in a flash that the superiority the British displayed in India was assumed, acquired from the exotic setting, like their tan" (253). The initial apathy which results from this realization is quickly transformed into a desire to test the superiority of the rulers.

It is Jerbanoo who takes it upon herself to subject the British she encounters to a set of trials. When, for example, Mrs Allen fails to perform according to the expected norms, Jerbanoo herself assumes the role of the tyrant. Her assumption is that if the British can no longer rule, they must be ruled by those more competent; the need for a dominant power is deeply-ingrained; "Poor Mrs Allen, closeted with Jerbanoo while the household frolicked about London, received the full blast of her scorn. Jerbanoo felt it demeaning to address such an inconsequential person as 'Mrs Allen,' and took to calling her hostess 'May-ree.' Mr Allen became 'Charlie'" (254–55). The ensuing confrontations become a battle of wits in which neither side can claim victory. The British are horrified by Jerbanoo's seemingly unpredictable behaviour, while Jerbanoo becomes increasingly disenchanted with her experience of England.

What Sidhwa criticizes in the Parsis is their acquiescence to being "Orientalized." When it becomes evident that the British are to leave India, the Parsis reorient themselves and once again submit themselves to the powers-to-be: "We will stay where we are . . . let Hindus, Muslims, Sikhs, or whoever, rule. What does it matter? The sun will continue to rise—and the sun will continue to set—in their arses . . .!" (283). Like Hedayat and Pezeshkzad, Sidhwa believes that the fate of the Parsis as "subjects" is, at least, partially a consequence of their willingness to accept and even create cultural stereotypes. As she does not foresee changes in the traditional attitudes of the Parsis,[12] she, too, is reluctant to predict new modes of exchange between East and West. In her interview with Jessica Greenbaum, Sidhwa speaks of the systematic self-imposed isolation of the Parsis, particularly among those who have emigrated to the United States. The same spirit of self-preservation, which once drove

---

[12] See Jessica Greenbaum's interview with Sidhwa "Minority of One," in *The Houstonian Magazine* June 1986: 50–2.

them from their native Iran to India, is now threatening their survival as a minority in the Western world. Sidhwa's own disaffection with the orthodox Parsis of North America is indicative of her distrust of simple cultural alliances.

In his short story, "Civilization's Spare Part," the Turkish satirist Aziz Nesin is less concerned with cultural exchanges between East and West than with the influence of imported Western technology. Yet, as hinted in the title of the story, the use or misuse of Western technology has clear implications for the culture of Turkey and, by extension, that of other Eastern nations.

The story, in some ways, echoes the Iranian writer Jalal Al-e Ahmad's treatise *Plagued by the West* (to be examined in the next chapter); it actualizes Al-e Ahmad's fears of the Third World's total dependence on Western machinery. The protagonist, Hamit Agha, once a successful farmer, is brought to ruin, when under pressure from relatives preoccupied with modernization, he replaces his old methods of farming with modern ones:

> When my son returned from the army, he said, "Father, I learned how to drive. Let us buy a tractor," he insisted. Just then my daughter came to the village with her husband . . . They too kept bothering me to buy a tractor. "Children, what would be the good of it? Aren't two pair of oxen enough?" They say I am backward-minded. My daughter pointed to the calendar page on the wall. "Look, father," she said. "We're in the year 1955. This is the twentieth century, did you know that?" My son-in-law gives an hour-long speech after every meal. "We are in the machine age. To plow with a pair of oxen is a disgrace these days."[13]

This obsession with the purchase of the tractor exhibits the symptoms of what Al-e Ahmad has called Westitis, or the need to indiscriminately mimic the West. In retrospect, Hamit Agha admits to having succumbed to pressure from his family because he did not wish to single himself out as the only farmer in the neighbourhood without a tractor: "I was exhausted by the nagging in the house, 'I'll buy it,' I said. Since even Memish Hüseyin had bought one, why should I be behind everybody?" (194)

---

[13] Janet Heineck, trans., "Civilization's Spare Part," in *An Anthology of Modern Turkish Short Stories*, ed Fahir Iz (Chicago and Minneapolis: Bibliotheca Islamica, 1978) 193–4.

The disastrous outcome of the purchase can, on the one hand, be attributed to the Turkish farmer's lack of appreciation of "the machine." Hamit Agha continues to equate the tractor with his oxen, endows it with a personality, and expects it to perform in the same manner:

> "If it were an Arab horse, it would be dying of exhaustion. This monster structure, this infidel invention—did you think it was an Arab horse?" We push, but it doesn't move. Like a donkey that sees water, it doesn't stir from its spot. How I missed the black ox! When you told it, "Come on, go!" it would uproot rock and mountain to go. (197)

When the tractor breaks down and needs spare parts, Hamit Agha expects to have to replace it as if it were one of his oxen. His attitude confirms his earlier suspicion that the new machinery only disrupts the well-established routine of the past. In other words, his failure to integrate the old and the new ways is to be attributed to his unwillingness to change and to adapt.

On the other hand, and this is a more serious charge against the East, Hamit Agha's problems are to blamed on the lack of a coherent system which would provide a smooth transition from the old to the new. The government agencies which all too eagerly endorse Hamit Agha's bank loans, and put him hopelessly in debt, are ill prepared for maintaining the machinery:

> A screw fell out—five hundred *liras*. A thousand *liras* for a part the size of a finger. A bolt comes loose—a thousand *liras*. Its chain breaks. Spare parts couldn't be found. A patch here, a patch there. That blessed tractor started to look like my trousers. While it plowed the ground, it shook all over like someone who has malaria. Everywhere in our field one can find a screw, a bolt, an iron bar, a shaft, or a chain. (197)

Even more incriminating is the government's approach to the problems of modernization. While the tractors are available for sale to Turkish farmers, the spare parts and the experts to work on them have to be brought from the West: "'We have ordered it from America. Until it comes, we are setting up a factory here, too. Wait a bit. We'll be turning out parts like rain.' Said he. 'I can't wait, but the bank can't wait. You tell the bank to wait.' Said I" (198). In this manner, not only the farmers but also the entire nation become increasingly dependent upon the West without having an alternative. The solution Aziz Nesin's protagonist finds is, in fact, a rejection of all attempts to fuse together Turkish farm life and Western technological advances:

> ... I could see that it wouldn't work. I gathered my son, daughter, son-in-law, and wife. "Come on, folks," said I, "let me show you how to repair this thing." I picked up a sledgehammer. I drove those people of mine like a flock of sheep. We came to the wreck. I struck the steering wheel and said, "Take *that*, you twentieth century," I struck the engine and said, "Take *that*, civilization." I struck the driving wheel with the sledgehammer and said, "Take *that*. This is your spare part." (198)

By underlining Hamit Agha's relief in the final episode, "It's as though I've been born again" (199), Aziz Nesin heightens the irony of the fate of others who are still bound to their slave-like dependence on the West. At the same time, the ending Aziz Nesin suggests is far from being satisfactory; Hamit Agha's actions are obviously self-destructive. By ridiculing the façade of westernization in Turkey, Nesin exposes the makeshift nature of Turkish-Western relations. Yet, Nesin is most critical of his own nation's naïve and blind acceptance of Western norms. He seems to suggest that interactions between East and West are doomed to failure as long as old structures and traditions remain unchanged.

The cynicism of Hedayat, Pezeshkzad, Sidhwa and Nesin reflects deeply-rooted problems which cannot be easily dismissed or overcome. Far from undermining challenges to Western stereotypes of the East, these writers are reluctant to find blame only in the West. They insist that new relations cannot be achieved by merely reversing the old approaches. They also call for an intense self-examination on the part of the East. In this sense, they are not unlike the other Eastern writers and scholars who advocate change, but they are more cautious and pragmatic in their approach. This need for pragmatism becomes evident as we turn to the last and the most vehement form of responses to the West.

Chapter Six

Some "Neo-Islamic" Responses

> The misfortunes of Islamic governments have come from the interference by foreigners in their destinies . . . It is America that considers the Koran and Islam to be harmful to itself and wishes to remove them from its way; it is America that considers Muslim men of religion a thorn in its path.[1]
>
> (Ayatollah Khomeini)

Eastern polemic against Western influence has sometimes led to a quest for an absolute alternative—most often found in the unifying message of Islam. In recent years, the term Islamic fundamentalism has become associated with defiance of the West, though to be sure the search for a collective identity in Islam partially corresponds to the Western nostalgia for its own lost empire. In Asad Abu Khalil's words, the sentiments underlying Islamic fundamentalism are in fact a form of neo-Orientalism, ascribing all identity to Islam just as many Western Orientalists have done: "According to this paradigm, Arabs are first and foremost Muslims. All ideological and political positions derive from sectarian affiliations. Socioeconomic and political differences are irrelevant."[2] Others, like Said, view the resurgence of Islam, in its new political dimension, only as a reaction to the ways in which the Islamic East has been treated by the West: ". . . I believe that even if we do not blame everything that is unhealthy about the Islamic world on the West, we must be able to see the connection between what the West has been

---

[1] Qtd. in Mottahedeh 246.
[2] Asad Abu Khalil, "Review of Fouad Ajami's *The Vanished Imam: Musa al Sadr and the Shiah of Lebanon*," *Middle East Report* January–February 1987: 46.

saying about Islam and what, reactively, various Muslim societies have done."[3]

One most interesting instance of Islamic riposte to Western imperialism can be found in one of Ayatollah Ruhollah Khomeini's earliest sermons, an act of defiance which led to his exile and subsequent emergence as the leader of the Iranian revolution. In 1964 the Iranian government asked the parliament to approve a bill giving American military advisers, their support staff, and their families posted in Iran diplomatic immunity. The original request was issued by the American government shortly before a large American loan was to be granted to Iran. The bill was passed with great reluctance and sparked off a range of emotional responses within the country. Among the figures who openly spoke against the passing of the bill was Khomeini. The text of the speech he gave on that occasion deserves critical attention if only as the prototype of a particular genre of anti-Orientalist treatises:

> Does the Iranian nation know what has happened in recent days in the Assembly? Does it know what crime has occurred surreptitiously and without the knowledge of the nation? Does it know that the Assembly, at the initiative of the government, has signed the document of the enslavement of Iran? It has acknowledged that Iran is a colony; it has given America a document attesting that the nation of Muslims is barbarous, it has struck out all our Muslim and national glories with a black line. By this shameful vote, if an American adviser or the servant of an American adviser should take any liberty with one of the greatest specialists in Shiah law . . . the police would have no right to arrest the perpetrator and the courts of Iran have no right to investigate. If the Shah should run over an American dog, he would be called to account but if an American cook should run over the Shah, no one has any claims against him . . . I proclaim that this shameful vote of the Majles is in contradiction to Islam and has no legality.[4]

It is significant that Khomeini's criticism of the bill focuses upon the opposition between Islam and the West; the restoration of "Iranian identity" is posited as a religious rather than a national duty. Khomeini suggests that it is incumbent on Iranian nationalists, opposed to this act of colonization, to be good Muslims. In Khomeini's statement, there-

---
[3] *Covering Islam* XVI.
[4] Qtd. in Mottahedeh 245–46. The epigraph to this chapter is also derived from this quotation.

fore, a legitimate claim against American domination in Iran is transformed into a global Islamic protest.

Such appeals were not always made by members of the clergy. Two of the most-renowned proponents of the revival of Islamic identity in Iran, Jalal Al-e Ahmad and Ali Shariati, were writers and ideologues who had extensive contact with the West. Although Al-e Ahmad was raised in a traditional Shi'ite family (both his father and his elder brother were clergymen), he drifted away from the family vocation. Initially he was sent to a religious school, but he enrolled himself in night courses administered by the Ministry of Education. Later he attended the Teachers College in Tehran and obtained a teaching certificate. Like many of his contemporaries, Al-e Ahmad was drawn into leftist political organizations of the time. For a period he joined the Iranian Communist Party and contributed to their publications. Disenchanted with the party's blatant pro-Soviet stance he then abandoned his official role within the party and directed his attention to a career as a writer and educator. In both endeavours he showed a preoccupation with the problems of the Iranian society, most of which he attributed to a naïve appreciation and adoption of Western standards.

His most influential work, *Gharbzadegi*,[5] originally published in 1962 as part of a report submitted to the Council on the Educational Goals of Iran, consists of an analysis of Iran's technological and intellectual dependence upon the West. Using the "machine" as a metaphor for the industrial and imperial expansion of the West, he argues that Iran and other developing countries have not effectively confronted Western influence. This condition, which he calls the disease of "Westitis," threatens the essence of all such societies:

> The basic point of this book is that we have not been able to preserve our "cultural-historical" personality in the face of the machine and its unavoidable onslaught. Rather we have been crushed by events. The point is that we have not been able to maintain a well-thought-out and considered position vis-à-vis this monster of the modern age. The fact is that until we have

---

[5] This title has been translated in English as "Plagued by the West," "Euromania," "Westomania," and "the disease of Westernism." In his translation, *Plagued by the West*, Bibliotheca Persica: Modern Persian Literature Series, 4 (Delmar, New York: Caravan, 1982), Paul Sprachman discusses the difficulties of translating the original Persian title.

actually grasped the essence, basis, and philosophy of western civilization and no longer superficially mimic the West in our consumption of western products, we shall be just like the ass who wore a lion skin. And we know what happened to him. (7)

Al-e Ahmad also bemoans the lack of religious sentiment on the part of Iranians: "The mosques and the pulpit are almost obsolete and if not completely so, are only needed during the days of Moharram and Ramazan" (44). This particular symptom of the Iranian dilemma receives more attention in Al-e Ahmad's discussion, for he believes that religion provides a remedy to the condition inflicted upon Iranian society. Like Khomeini, he regards Islam, or at least Shi'ism, as a political and ideological force capable of reshaping and unifying Iranian society. Had Al-e Ahmad lived to see the outcome of his own predictions in the Iranian revolution, he may have tempered his optimism. Traditionally Iranians, with their brand of Islam, have not been able to endear themselves to the rest of the Islamic world. The Iranian revolution, instead of uniting Iran and other Islamic nations, has led to the further isolation of Iran in the Islamic world. In their first application, it would seem, Al-e Ahmad's abstractions have fallen short of his expectations.

Although Al-e Ahmad holds Iranians themselves responsible for the spread of "Westitis," he is equally critical of Western scholars, sarcastically referred to as "our gentlemen Orientalists," who helped to pave the way for the cultural subjugation of the East. Like Said, Al-e Ahmad sees Orientalism as a politically motivated phenomenon. He, too, questions its validity as a science. Yet Al-e Ahmad's skepticism runs deeper than Said's:

> Since when has orientalism become a "science"? If we say that some westerner is a linguist or a dialectologist or a musicologist in the oriental field, that is something else again. Or if we say that he is an anthropologist or a sociologist, that is even possible. But an orientalist in a general sense? What does that mean? Does it mean that he knows all the secrets of the East? Are we living in the age of Aristotle? This is why I call orientalism a parasitic growth on the roots of imperialism. What is really amusing is that these orientalists have organizations affiliated with UNESCO, biennial and quadrennial congresses, gatherings and such nonsense. (73)

Al-e Ahmad's argument becomes contradictory when, on the one hand, he insists on the incompatibility of the imported Western norms and the prescribed Shi'ite code of conduct, but, on the other hand, suggests that the East's material dependence on the West be remedied through the adoption of Western models for industrial growth and self-sufficiency.

In his encounter with the West, however, Al-e Ahmad found it necessary to modify some of his earlier suppositions. He altered the tone and the content of his treatise on westernization when he was given a chance to present it to a Western audience. The setting was the 1965 Harvard International Summer Seminar directed by Henry Kissinger to which Al-e Ahmad was invited. No longer concerned with the identity of individual nations, he now advocated the primacy of a world culture. Some have argued that this radical change in perspective was partly due to the intimidating setting of his presentation.[6] However eager Al-e Ahmad may have been to adapt his doctrine for the American audience, he did not succeed in gaining their appreciation. After his return to Iran he reverted to his initial position, which was now being taken up by other intellectuals. He found himself a leading figure in a movement which Ali Shariati referred to as the cultural decolonization of Iran.

Shariati, like Jalal Al-e Ahmad, came from a devout Muslim background. His education, however, was completed in France where he obtained a doctorate in sociology in 1965. This period of his life in France was to have a strong influence in his philosophical orientation; he was brought into contact with the works of Sartre and Frantz Fanon, and introduced to the ideology of the Algerian liberation movement. In Fanon's treatises, especially, Shariati found a framework for his own approach: "By expounding certain theories of Fanon, which previously had been almost entirely unknown, and translating some of the conclusions in his book, Shariati enabled the echo of Fanon's thought and outlook to reach the Iranian popular movement of which he was part."[7]

After his return to Iran, Shariati became a lecturer at a religious meeting hall. His popular and well-attended lectures addressed issues of cultural and sociological import. He made ample use of his knowledge of Western philosophies. Fusing them together with Shi'ite ideology, he

---

[6] For further details see Mottahedeh 321–22.
[7] Hamid Algar, trans., "Introduction to *On the Sociology of Islam: Lectures*," (Berkeley: Mizan, 1979) 23.

attempted to offer an alternative to the dogmatism of the Shi'ite clergy. In a manner similar to Al-e Ahmad, he encouraged Iranian identification with Islam:

> Since World War II, many intellectuals in the Third World, whether religious or non-religious, have stressed that their societies must return to their roots and rediscover their history, their culture, and their popular language . . . Some of you may conclude that we Iranians must return to our racial roots. I categorically reject this conclusion. I oppose racism, fascism and reactionary returns. Moreover, Islamic civilization has worked like scissors and has cut us off from our pre-Islamic past . . . For us to return to our roots means not a rediscovery of pre-Islamic Iran, but a return to our Islamic, especially Shiah roots.[8]

Nevertheless, he believed that the doctrines of Islam should be reinterpreted and adapted to the needs of contemporary societies. He defined this approach as "new originality," or "means of finding appropriate models for each society."[9] Such means were sometimes found in unlikely juxtapositions of Western and Eastern ideologies, as demonstrated in a title like *Red Shi'ism*. In "Approaches to the Understanding of Islam," his discussion is couched in terms which reflect his affinity with certain Western schools of thought: "Islam, as a scientific school of sociology, believes that social change and development cannot be based on accident, for society is a living organism, possessed of immutable and scientifically demonstrable norms. Further, man possesses liberty and free will . . ."[10] Or, in the essay "The Philosophy of History: Cain and Abel," he integrates a refutation of Freud into his analysis:

> It is all this that makes of Cain . . . a creature ready to lie, to commit treachery, to drag his faith into the mud with a quiet conscience, and ultimately to behead his brother, all for the sake of his sexual inclinations—not even some crazed and powerful infatuation, but straightforward and transient lust! No, Mr. Freud, he does all these things not because his sexual instincts are stronger than those of others, but because human virtues have grown exceedingly weak in him. (106)

As once again demonstrated in the doctrines of the Iranian revolution,

---

[8] Qtd. in Mottahedeh 330–31.
[9] Ali Shariati, *History of Civilization*, Vol. II (Tehran: Agah, 1983) 262.
[10] *On the Sociology of Islam* 52.

these treatises were not without some obvious contradictions. The Islamic Republic has used Islam as anything but a "scientific school of sociology," nor has it embraced the principles of "liberty and free will." It is with reason that, in a survey of the works of Muslim reformists, Fouad Ajami has called into question Shariati's utopian method of effecting social and political change:

> All along, men like Shariati . . . had been playing with fire. They had assumed that Islam could be unleashed to bring down the old order and that its passion could be harnessed to build something decent and pretty. They had assigned to that Islamic force an "anti-imperialist" function. In their fantasy, Islam would bring down a political world tied to the power of the foreigners, and then it would blow over.[11]

Shariati's career and his ambitions are repeated in the life and works of another Iranian Shi'ite ideologue, imam Musa al Sadr, who succeeded in exporting his ideas to Lebanon. Like Shariati, he "had a 'soft' modernist reading of the Shiah faith. His early discourses in [Lebanon], the ideas that attracted attention, that brought him fame and influential followers, were reiterations of the old themes of 'Muslim modernism.'"[12]

In his lectures and sermons, like Shariati, Musa al Sadr often gave vehement responses to Western scholarship on the Islamic East: "He quoted and rebutted the Orientalist Sir Hamilton Gibb on the compatibility between Islam and modern ideas; he ranged over Islamic history to note contributors to science and philosophy. It was a tour de force that came straight out of the literature of Islamic modernism."[13] Ironically, however, it was in the East that Musa al Sadr was perceived as a threat. Although, unlike Shariati and Al-e Ahmad, Musa al Sadr had the opportunity to carry out some of his theories in Lebanon, he came up against resistance by the more orthodox forces of Islam. His mysterious disappearance in Libya is a reminder of the internal rivalries of the Muslim East. It is also a symbol for the failure of the so-called modernist reforms to be integrated into the canon.

---

[11] Fouad Ajami, "The Doctrines of Ali Shariati and their Defeat: The Impossible Life of Muslim Liberalism," *The New Republic* 2 June 1986: 31.

[12] Fouad Ajami, *The Vanished Imam: Musa al Sadr and the Shiah of Lebanon* (Ithaca: Cornell University Press, 1986) 89.

[13] Ibid. 91.

The movement that swept pre-revolutionary Iran, its contradictions, notwithstanding, must be looked upon as an effective challenge to Western perception and treatment of the Islamic Orient. Its mere historical presence has determined the course of many academic studies of the nature of East-West relations. Abu Khalil's term, neo-Orientalism, may not present an accurate and comprehensive description of a school of thought. Nevertheless, it provides a framework for understanding publications such as *Orientalism, Islam, and Islamists*. Acknowledging their indebtedness to Said, the authors of this volume strongly suggest that Orientalism, and by extension Western imperialism, stem exclusively from an inadequate understanding of Islam. In an introductory statement, the editors adopt the rhetoric and the logic of religious believers:

> Orientalism, hopelessly insensitive to the feelings of Muslims, ignores as of no consequence the historical fact of Muslim belief in Islam; whatever the Orientalists' belief, their belief remains a fact. In insisting, first, that "Islam" is a cultural artifact, and then judging it against Western norms, the Orientalists miss the cultural fact that, for Muslims, Islam is primarily an ongoing concern to live in submission to the will of God, and they miss, too, an occasion to contribute intelligently to that concern.[14]

Too often the essayists resort to the perspective of a "devout" Muslim. In "Bernard Lewis and Islamic Studies: An Assessment," for example, Sulayman S. Nyang and Samir Abed-Rabbo attempt to discredit the classical Orientalist by merely citing his former institutional affiliations: "While at London University he operated as an intelligence agent of the British foreign office; at Princeton his works seem to be designed to generate and sustain support for Israel. This is a fact which any investigator willing to trace Lewis's biographical steps will see for himself" (279). In "Alongsidedness-in Good Faith? An Essay on Kenneth Cragg," Jamil Qureshi goes so far as to suggest that only the adoption of Islam as a world religion would eliminate the disparities between East and West. The underlying argument appears to be that Orientalism must be replaced by Islam: "Whether Islam may draw and rescue Western nonbelief (no longer confined to the West) is not an easy question. It depends

---

[14] Asaf Hussain, Robert Olson, Jamil Qureshi, eds. *Orientalism, Islam, Islamists* (Brattleboro, Vermont: Amana, 1984) 2.

upon whether non-believers will feel drawn to the way committed Muslims actually live, which means getting to know them" (249). Such utopian visions can be seen as extensions of the doctrines of Shariati and Al-e Ahmad; Islam is the answer not only to the dilemma of the East but also to the disillusionment of the West.[15] As a result, what initially reads like a defence of Islam soon becomes an Islamic offensive. The alternative offered by the essays to the Eurocentric or Orientalist discourse is a radical one, that of the worldwide hegemony of Islam.

The belief in the universal "healing" power of Islam has, in spite of its currency in the Islamic East, surprisingly few reflections in fiction. Its doctrinal nature does not easily lend itself to subtle fictional representation. In her novel, *Foreigner*, published shortly before the Iranian revolution, the Iranian writer Nahid Rachlin echoes the prevalent sentiments of the time, especially among Iranians who after years of living in the West returned to Iran to be swallowed up by the new religious fervour. The protagonist of Rachlin's novel, Feri, once in Iran begins to shed her adopted American identity. As her American husband fades in her memory, she is ever more drawn to the primitive life offered by her religious relatives. It is on a visit to a shrine that Feri undergoes the final transformation:

> The wall around the sarcophagus of the saint and all the other walls were covered with silver circular knobs. People walked around, kissing the walls, whispering prayers and crying. Echoes, faraway, vibrated in my head, my whole body. Surges of memory, of going from chamber to chamber in mosques and shrines, clinging to my mother, flowed over the surface of my mind. Suddenly, in spite of myself, I stopped, leaned my head against a wall and kissed it, tears filling my eyes rolling down my cheeks.[16]

Feri's sudden and uncritical self-abandonment, incongruous with her

---

[15] Al-e Ahmad concludes *Plagued by the West* by summing up his impressions of the current despair into which Western metaphysics has fallen: "I see that Albert Camus and Eugène Ionesco and Ingmar Bergman and many other artists (all of them from the West) have become apostles of this message of resurrection. All of them have given up on the future of mankind . . . I understand all of these fictional destinies to be omens, foreboding the Hour of Judgment, warning that the machine demon if not harnessed and put back into the bottle, will place a hydrogen bomb at the end of the road for mankind" (111). Faced with this universal cataclysm, Al-e Ahmad returns to the Koran, positing it as the saviour of humanity.

[16] Nahid Rachlin, *Foreigner* (New York: W. W. Norton, 1978) 125.

training as a research scientist, leads to romantic visions of a simple life of harmony: "I zigzagged through the people and tress . . . No one noticed me. I was an Iranian woman, wearing a *chador*" (190). These naïve resolutions do not shield her against a reality, less tainted with primitivism, which must nevertheless be confronted: "I turned over and looked at my mother. Her face was serene in her sleep. I knew soon I would have to make decisions, think beyond the day, but for the moment I lay there. Tranquil" (192). Although this last sentence of the novel is not indicative of a development in the character of the protagonist, it underlines the temporariness of her self-discovery. Even in this fictional setting, an undisturbed and unproblematic fusing of East and West through Islam becomes doubtful.

One of the contemporary critics who has attempted to come to terms with ethnocentrism in the discourse of both the East and the West is Abdelkebir Khatibi. Citing Fanon's call for an alternative mode of response in the opening passage of *Maghreb pluriel,* Khatibi sets the tone for the series of essays which follow: "Allons, camarades, le jeu européen est définitivement terminé, il faut trouver autre chose" (11). In Khatibi's view, this other perspective can only be realized through a critical re-examination of all cultural biases. He perceives a coincidence between decolonization and "deconstruction"—one which needs to be further exploited for the creation of a new self-image in the East:

> Du point de vue de ce qu'on appelle encore le Tiers Monde, nous ne pouvons prétendre que la décolonisation a pu promouvoir une pensée radicalement critique vis-à-vis de la machine idéologique de l'impérialisme et de l'ethnocentrisme, une décolonisation qui serait en même temps une déconstruction des discours qui participent, de manières variées et plus ou moins dissimulées, à la domination impériale, qui est entendue ici également dans son pouvoir de parole. Oui, nous ne sommes pas arrivés à cette décolonisation de pensée qui serait, au-delà d'un renversement de ce pouvoir, l'affirmation d'une différence, une subversion absolue et libre de l'esprit. Il y a là comme un vide, un intervalle silencieux entre le fait de la colonisation et celui de la décolonisation. (47–8)

Khatibi further suggests that an alternative to ethnocentrism, be it Eastern or Western, cannot be found within one given ideological, historical, or cultural setting. Rather, it is an ongoing process of critical analysis directed both inward and outward—what he refers to as the notion of *double critique*: "La double critique consiste à opposer à l'épistème occidentale son dehors impensé tout en radicalisant la marge, non seulement dans une *pensée en arabe*, mais dans une pensée autre qui parle *en langues*, se mettant à l'écoute de toute parole d'où qu'elle vienne" (63).

A pragmatic application of this concept in North Africa would undermine the possibility of recapturing a unified past: "Il n'y a pas de retour en soi, rien, rien que des transformations critiques, selon notre perspective" (24), and instead promote a plurality of many already present identities and voices: "Il faudrait penser le Maghreb tel qu'il *est*, site topographique entre l'Orient, l'Occident et l'Afrique, et tel qu'il puisse se mondialiser pour son propre compte" (38–9). Khatibi's vision requires an element of dynamic change which must originate from within.

At least on a theoretical level, Khatibi has been successful in moving beyond the initial stage of either rhetorical responses to Orientalism or recommendations for the replacement of one cultural hegemony with another. He best captures the nature of a movement in progress by suggesting that there may not yet exist the possibility of "eliminating East and West altogether," but that there is the beginning of a critical apparatus for dealing with encounters between East and West.

Conclusion

> The tyranny of silence shall be broken—
> New shining words by us, the poets, spoken;
> Whereas a diver threads dull pearls upon a string
> We choose the words which soar—and give them wing.[1]
>
> (Qulzum)

The works examined in this study bear witness to the fallacy of the image of a reticent Orient. As seen in the previous chapters, Eastern writers and scholars have indeed realized and acted upon the need to come to terms with the West and, even more importantly, with Western perceptions of themselves. Weighed against the outwardly directed challenges of scholars like Said and Kabbani, the introspection and self-questionings of writers like Hedayat and Rushdie are equally significant and necessary attempts at redefining the position of the East vis-à-vis the West. Whether this trend towards redefining the parameters of the study of the Islamic East will gain the type of institutional support enjoyed by the discipline of Orientalism remains to be seen. At present, however, the movement faces major obstacles both within itself and in its reception in the West.

For the most part, Eastern scholars have abandoned the singularity of vision with which some traditional Orientalists approach the study of the East. This expansion of perspective has certainly created an atmosphere more conducive to cross-cultural studies. But in the multiplicity of voices heard there are hints of discord and internal strife. I have referred to, especially in chapter six, the militant branch of the movement whose ultimate representative is the Iranian revolution—perhaps, in its vociferous challenges, also one of the most effective forms of response to the West. For this reason, the course of its development can shed light on the direction of the future interactions between the Middle East and the West. Still misunderstood in the West as a form of religious fanaticism,

---

[1] J. C. E. Owen, trans., *Modern Islamic Literature from 1800 to the Present* 181.

the Iranian revolution has, nevertheless, forced many "specialists" to reconsider their preconceptions of the Muslim East. In this particular case, at least, the East had demonstrated an ability to challenge the West and pose itself as a threat. By the same token, however, the confrontational attitudes of the most vehement revolutionaries has widened the gulf between East and West.

After an initial phase during which a larger segment of the Iranian intelligentsia embraced the revolutionary ideals, the Iranian revolution has failed to attract supporters among moderates either in the East or in the West. Born out of deep-seated and legitimate resentments, the revolution has created its own set of stereotypes of the West. Labels such as the "Great Satan" and the "decadent West" naturally come to mind. Such slogans are integral to a movement of this nature and magnitude, but they also have the power to undermine the very goals of the revolution.

An interesting example of the internal contradictions brought about by such rhetoric was unfolded in two consecutive issues of the Islamic Republic's official literary magazine, *Kayhan-e Farhangi* (*The Cultural Kayhan*). In its November 1986 issue, an article was devoted to Wole Soyinka's winning of the Nobel Prize. Soyinka was hailed as a "Third-World" writer committed "to the cause of the oppressed."[2] In the next issue, however, one of the readers objected to the journal's admitting Soyinka to the ranks of committed writers precisely because he has received recognition from the West. The letter to the editor reads:

> Let us not forget that the Nobel Prize has traditionally been awarded to a select group of people—certainly not those who have distanced themselves from Western imperialism. Need I remind your readers that Soyinka is a Protestant who sided against his Muslim brothers during the Biafran War? He was also imprisoned during the same period as a traitor. Moreover, as a writer he has turned away from the traditions of his own people: instead of Yoruba or Arabic, a language accessible to a larger segment of the population of the African continent, he has chosen to write in English. I do not wish to belittle Soyinka's literary endeavors or call into question the merits of the Nobel Prize. On the contrary, I welcome the possibility of a fair competition between Western writers and their Muslim counterparts. Yet I

---

[2] "Notes and Remarks," *Kayhan-e Farhangi* 3 (November 1986): 43–4.

hesitate to share your enthusiasm. Were Begin and Sadat not among winners of the Nobel Prize?[3]

Soyinka, whose works have been of interest to the readers of *Kayhan-e Farhangi*, must necessarily be chastised, once he has been identified with the West. Similar reasoning was brought to bear against the Egyptian writer Naguib Mahfouz after he won the Nobel Prize. Some thirty years after the initial publication and banning of his controversial novel,[4] Mahfouz is now the target of renewed attacks whose aims are to construct an image of the Islamic world. Islam is to be seen as an active method of counteracting westernization; as soon as Mahfouz has gained recognition in the West, he must be denounced for facilitating an alliance between his own culture and the West: "Asked why Mahfouz is being threatened for a novel published so long ago, radical Muslim leader Alaa Mohieddin said it was because the author is now famous as a Nobel prize winner."[5] The Muslim leader quoted in this statement may have intended to convey a sense of his duty to correct misrepresentations of Islam, but, unwittingly, he reveals his propagandist intentions. This deliberate and careful distortion of "reality" is worthy of the label "Islamist discourse." Its manifestation in the case of the publication of Salman Rushdie's *The Satanic Verses* may be a troubling reminder of the consistency of all discourse.

The crisis surrounding Salman Rushdie's novel is, in fact, a touchstone for many aspects of the phenomenon I have been describing. The book and the responses it has generated in the Muslim world display the full range of interactions between the Middle East and the West, to say nothing of the interactions within the Muslim world.

Many commentators have attempted to reduce this crisis to a simple opposition, reminiscent of Hegel's dichotomy, between the principles of

---

[3] Seyyed Mohammad Ali Sajjadieh, "How The Nobel Prize is Granted," *Kayhan-e Farhangi* 3 (December 1986): 36. The translation is my own and has also appeared in "Iranian Reflections on Soyinka," in *African Literature Association Bulletin* 13.4 (Spring 1987): 10–11.

[4] When Mahfouz first published *Children of Gabalawi* in serial form, al-Azhar succeeded in having it banned in 1969.

[5] Lachlan Carmichael, "Nobel Laureate Faces Threats for Novel 'Offensive' to Islam," *The Globe and Mail* 28 April 1989: A16.

the freedom of the individual in the West and dogmatic religiosity in the Islamic East. This type of interpretation falls within the realm of the binary oppositions we have seen in the previous chapters, i.e. Oriental/ Occidental and self/other. Unfortunately, this logic obscures many significant factors in the so-called Rushdie affair. As I have demonstrated, examples of religious and political satire exist in modern Middle Eastern literatures and they are but the most recent instances of the tradition of dissidence in Arab and other Islamic literatures.[6] They may have met with censorship, as in the case of Tāhā Husain or Sadegh Hedayat, yet they have survived the initial outcry. But Rushdie's novel has become a ploy in the manipulation of public opinion both in the Islamic world and the West. The events surrounding the publication of *The Satanic Verses* may be interpreted on at least three different levels: 1) The Iranian authorities, who only became interested in the book after the well-publicized demonstrations in Britain, may have used the incident to ally themselves more closely with other Muslim nations—this at a time Iran has been suffering from global isolation. 2) The denunciation of Rushdie may have been considered a means of rallying the masses, highly-demoralized after the inconclusive end of the Iran-Iraq war. 3) Much of the official Iranian rhetoric was obviously directed at the West. That Rushdie, as someone from an Islamic background, could publish a blasphemous book in the West was interpreted, at least publicly, as a threat to the very essence of any Islamic state.

The intricate calculations behind the Iranian reaction to Rushdie's book, however, should not be seen as completely divorced from Rushdie's own manipulations, although their fictionality further removes them from every-day concerns. As it is clear in Rushdie's previous works, he constantly juxtaposes and rewrites the traditions with which he has come into contact. His first novel, *Grimus*, is, as we saw above, exemplary of this type of creativity. But Rushdie's imaginative rep-

[6] As Jamel Eddine Bencheikh has pointed out, dissidence and its reflections in literature are, in fact, integral to the tradition of Islamic literature and should not be regarded as a new phenomenon: "Si nous acceptons cela aujourd'hui, il faudra en toute logique regarder de plus près quelques glorieuses pages de la littérature arabe. Il faudra passer en jugement Bashshâr, Abû Nuwâs, Mutî', Ibn al-Muqaffa', Abû l-'Alâ' l-Ma'arrî, al-Hallâdj, Ibn Quzmân, et quelques dizaines d'autres. Il faudra de nouveau bannir, Ibn Rushd, Ibn Bâdja et quelques philosophes." "Islam et Littérature," *Le Monde* 7 April 1989: 17.

resentations are themselves to some extent distortions. In his novel *Shame*, there is an interesting instance of the way in which fiction may, intentionally or unintentionally, colour reality. In a passage related by the self-conscious narrator of *Shame* we read:

> May I interpose a few words here on the subject of the Islamic revival? It won't take long. Pakistan is not Iran. This may sound like a strange thing to say about the country which was, until Khomeini, one of the only two theocracies on earth (Israel being the other one), but it's my opinion that Pakistan has never been a mullah-dominated society . . . So-called Islamic "fundamentalism" does not spring, in Pakistan, from the people. It is imposed on them from above, (250–51)

In the world of fiction, we may overlook the narrator's naïve understanding of the sources of fundamentalism in Iran and Pakistan. Yet, the metafictional aspects of *Shame* draw us to a more critical examination of this statement. We may ask why fundamentalism manifests itself differently in Iran and Pakistan. Are the demonstrations against *The Satanic Verses* in Pakistan not a categorical rejection of the narrator/author's belief? The assumption made in the above statement is that because the present form of government in Iran emerged from a popular revolution it is, in all its manifestations, a true representative of the Iranian people. Conversely, theocracy in Pakistan, which resulted from a military coup and never received open popular support, should not be equated with the wishes of the majority in Pakistan. This misunderstanding of the importance and the role of mass movements in the shaping of history extends to a larger misinterpretation of the post-revolutionary nature of Iranian society. Although more harmless than the official Iranian simplification of the "message" of *The Satanic Verses*, Rushdie's pronouncements nevertheless exemplify the internal strifes of the Islamic world.

Particulary interesting to our discussion is the way in which both Rushdie and his opponents, in so far as they embody aspects of Islamic civilization, are engaged in a confrontation which draws in the Western world, be it as a mediator or a bystander. The positions adopted by both sides, therefore, also become defined in terms of the third participant. This constitutes a more subtle form of interaction between the two worlds which may, at some later stage, prove to be a source of innovation. For the moment the polarizations remain prominent.

CONCLUSION

For Rushdie and others in his position, self-definition demands a difficult and complex relationship between cultures. In his commentary on *The Satanic Verses*, the Iranian writer Taghi Modarressi, himself a cross-cultural writer, gives an interesting analysis of an aspect of Rushdie's dilemma not often discussed in the context of his novel:

> Living in a new world, as I do, I can lament my lost paradise, or I can try to fit into the new culture as best I can. Or I can do what Rushdie has done: I can be prankish, put on a clown show, dramatize my conflicts by distancing myself from my background. Then the audience will be enchanted by my flair and my exotic acrobatics, and I will finally shake off that awkward sense of being internally divided. The actor after all, stays above both cultures since his purpose is to conquer them, not to belong to them.[7]

If Rushdie's "acrobatics" allow him the kind of aloofness described by Modarressi, his Islamic opponents, be they residents of Western or Islamic countries, entrench themselves in what they assume to be their "authentic" culture. Both seem to be plagued by illusions which stem from a belief in clearly-defined and maintained boundaries between cultures. What Modarressi shows to be the dilemma of the immigrant writer—also echoed in Rushdie's own words in *Shame*: "It is generally believed that something is always lost in translation; I cling to the notion . . . that something can also be gained."(29)—is or should perhaps be the norm rather than the exception. My point is that cultures, nations, and identities are never defined in terms of simple binary oppositions—unless, of course, through the artifice of a "discourse." But if we see and fix everything within discursive frameworks, do we not deliberately obscure a pluralist vision which allows for more complex and less ethnocentric relations? I believe in an era of easy polarizations the complexities rather than the stereotypes should be delineated and emphasized. If, like Edward Said, we maintain that "the answer to Orientalism is not Occidentalism" (328), we must abandon the labels, more easily made than overcome, and examine both realms in an equal light. We may also have to adopt a critical perspective not only vis-à-vis others,

---

[7] Taghi Modarressi, "Salman Rushdie and the Immigrant's Dilemma," *The Washington Post* 12 March 1989: 7.

CONCLUSION

but ourselves. This means that in an impasse, such as the one in the case of *The Satanic Verses*, we not scurry back to familiar labels. Instead, we must expose the rhetoric which determines the nature and the course of the dilemma.

Systematic stereotyping of the West, or what one could call Occidentalism, does not exist in modern Eastern letters. There is rather a whole range of responses from the early travellers' distant admiration of the West, Tāhā Husain and Naïm Kattan's confrontation of their "other" in the West, Salman Rushdie and Taghi Modarressi's embracing of a double identity, Aziz Nesin and Sadegh Hedayat's ridicule of westernization, to the neo-Islamists's rejection of anything but the "authentic" self. This may be due to a lack of political power and institutional development in the Islamic East, but we must bear in mind that institutions do not absolutely define discourse—Western Orientalism was capable of producing figures like Edward G. Browne who wrote:

> For Islam and the Perso-Arabian civilization of Islam I have the deepest admiration; an admiration which it is especially incumbent on me to confess at a time when they are so much misunderstood and misrepresented by Europeans; who appear to imagine that they themselves have a monopoly of civilization, and a kind of divine mandate to impose on the whole world not only their own political institutions but their own modes of thought.[8]

The alternative to Orientalism and Occidentalism may well lie in Khatibi's call to "listen to all discourse, wherever it originates,"[9] and to recognize how many places voices come from. Those who revert to the old paradigms may find themselves on the brink of the kind of madness described by T. E. Lawrence: " . . . and then madness was very near, as I believe it would be near the man who could see things through the veils at once of two customs, two educations, two environments."[10]

---

[8] Edward G. Browne, *A Literary History of Persia*, Vol. II (Cambridge: University Press, 1956) X.
[9] This is my own translation of a phrase previously quoted from *Maghreb pluriel* 63.
[10] *Seven Pillars of Wisdom*, seventh edition (London: Jonathan Cape, 1942) 30.

Bibliography

PRIMARY SOURCES

A) Fiction

Al-Shaykh, Hanan. *The Story of Zahra*. English translation by Readers International. London: Readers International 1986.
Boullata, Kamal. Ed. and trans. *Women of the Fertile Crescent: Modern Poetry by Arab Women*. 1978; Rpt. Washington, D.C.: Three Continents, 1981.
Chraïbi, Driss. *Les Boucs*. Paris: Denoël, 1955.
Hedayat, Sadegh. *The Blind Owl*. D. P. Costello, trans. New York: Grove, 1969.
———. "The Caravan of Islam." Paris: Organisation des mouvements nationalistes des universitaires, chercheurs et intellectuels iraniens, 1982.
Husain, Tāhā. *A Passage to France*. Trans. Kenneth Cragg. Arabic Translation Series, 4 Leiden: E. J. Brill, 1976.
Kattan, Naïm. *Adieu Babylone*. Montréal: La Presse, 1975.
———. *Les Fruits arrachés*. Montréal: Hurtubise, 1977.
———. "Le Gardien de l'alphabet." In *La Traversée*. Montréal: Hurtubise, 1976. 109–25.
Kritzeck, James. Ed. *Modern Islamic Literature from 1800 to the Present*. New York: Mentor, 1970.
Manzaloui, Mahmoud. Ed. *Arabic Short Stories 1945–1965*. Cairo: American University in Cairo Press, 1985.
Modarressi, Taghi. *The Book of Absent People*. New York: Doubleday, 1986.
Mukherjee, Bharati. *Darkness*. Markham, Ontario: Penguin, 1985.
——— and Clark Blaise. *Days and Nights in Calcutta*. New York: Doubleday, 1977.
———. *Wife*. Boston: Houghton Mifflin, 1972.
Nesin, Aziz. "Civilization's Spare Part." Trans. Janet Heineck. In *An Anthology of Modern Turkish Short Stories*. Ed. Fahir Iz. Minneapolis and Chicago: Bibliotheca Islamica, 1978. 193–99.
Pezeshkzad, Iraj. *My Dear Uncle Napoleon*. 1968; rpt. London: Paka, n.d.
Rachlin, Nahid. *Foreigner*. New York: W. W. Norton, 1978.
Rushdie, Salman. *Grimus*. 1975; rpt. London: Granada, 1982.
———. *Shame*. London: Jonathan Cape, 1983.
Salih, Tayeb. *Season of Migration to the North*. Trans. Denys Johnson-Davies. 1969; rpt. Washington D.C.: Three Continents, 1985.
Scheinhardt, Saliha. *Drei Zypressen*. Berlin: EXpress, 1984.
———. *Frauen, die sterben, ohne daß sie gelebt hätten*. Berlin: EXpress, 1983.
———. *Und die Frauen weinten Blut*. Berlin: EXpress, 1980.
Shirazi, Manny. *Javady Alley*. London: Women's Press, 1984.
Sidhwa, Bapsi. *The Crow Eaters*. New York: St. Martin's 1981.

B) Travelogues, Essays, and Scholarly Writing

Al-e Ahmad, Jalal. *Plagued by the West.* Trans. Paul Sprachman. Bibliotheca Persica: Modern Persian Literature Series, 4. Delmar, New York: Caravan, 1982.
Alloula, Malek. *The Colonial Harem.* Trans. Myrna Godzich and Wlad Godzich. Theory and History of Literature, 21. Minneapolis: University of Minnesota Press, 1986.
Defrémery, C. and B. R. Sanguinetti. Trans. and Ed. *Voyages d'Ibn Batouta, texte arabe accompagné d'une introduction.* Vol. IV. Paris: Imprimerie Nationale, 1879.
Hussain, Asaf. Robert Olson, and Jamil Qureshi. Eds. *Orientalism, Islam, and Islamists.* Brattleboro, Vermont: Amana, 1984.
Kabbani, Rana. *Europe's Myths of Orient.* Bloomington: Indiana University Press, 1986.
Kattan, Naïm. "Littérature de [sic] Québec: Langue et Identité." *Canadian Literature*, 58 (Autumn 1973): 61–3.
Khatibi, Abdelkebir. *Maghreb pluriel.* Paris: Denoël, 1983.
———. *La Mémoire tatouée.* Paris: Denoël, 1971.
Le Strange, G. Trans. and ed. *Don Juan of Persia: A Shiah Catholic.* Broadway Travellers Series. London: George Routledge, 1926.
Moser, Brigitte. *Die Chronik des Ahmed Sinân Celebi: gennant Bihisti: Eine Quelle zur Geschichte des Osmanischen Reiches unter Sultan Bâyezid II.* Beiträge zur Kenntnis Südosteuropas und des nahen Orients. München: Dr. Dr. Rudolf Trofenik, 1980.
Mukherjee, Bharati. "Mimcry and Reinvention." In *The Proceedings of the Second Triennial Conference of the Canadian Association for Commonwealth Language and Literature Studies.* Part II. Ed. Uma Parameswaran. Calcutta: Writers Workshop, 1983. 147–57.
Parathasarathy, R. "Whoring after English Gods." In *Writers in East-West Encounter: New Cultural Bearings.* Ed. Guy Amirthanayagam. London: Macmillan, 1982. 64–84.
Redhouse, J. W. Trans. *The Diary of H. M. The Shah of Persia During his Tour through Europe A. D. 1873.* London: John Murray, 1874.
Said, Edward W. *After the Last Sky: Palestinian Lives.* Photographs by Jean Mohr. New York: Pantheon, 1986.
———. *Covering Islam: How the Media and the Experts Determine How We See the Rest of the World.* New York: Pantheon, 1981.
———. *Orientalism.* 1978; rpt. New York: Vintage, 1979.
Said, Laila. *Bridge Through Time: A Memoir.* New York: Summit, 1985.
Shariati, Ali. *History of Civilization.* Vol. II. Tehran: Agah, 1983.
———. *On the Sociology of Islam: Lectures.* Trans. Hamid Algar. Berkeley: Mizan, 1979.
Tugay, Emine Foat. *Three Centuries: Family Chronicles of Turkey and Egypt.* London: Oxford University Press, 1963.

SECONDARY SOURCES

Abu-Khalil, Asad. "Review of Fouad Ajami's *The Vanished Imam: Musa al-Sadr and the Shiah of Lebanon.*" *Middle East Report*, January-February 1987: 46–7.
Abu-Lughod, Ibrahim. *Arab Rediscovery of Europe: A Study in Cultural Encounters.* Oriental Studies, 22. Princeton: University Press, 1963.
Ajami, Fouad. "The Doctrines of Ali Shariati and their Defeat: The Impossible Life of Muslim Liberalism." *The New Republic* 2 June 1986: 26–32.
———. *The Vanished Imam: Musa al Sadr and the Shia of Lebanon.* Ithaca: Cornell University Press, 1986.

Alavi, Bozorg. *Geschichte und Entwicklung der modernen persischen Literatur.* Berlin: Akademie, 1964.
Allard, Jacques. "Naïm Kattan ou la fortune du migrant." *Voix et Images* 11 (1985): 7–9.
——. "Entrevue avec Naïm Kattan." *Voix et Images* 11 (1985): 10–32.
Allen, Roger. *The Arabic Novel: An Historic and Critical Introduction.* Syracuse: Syracuse University Press, 1982.
Amprimoz, Alexandre. "Quebec Writers: The Anatomy of Solitude." *Tamarack Review* 72 (1977): 79–87.
Appenzell, Anthony. "Modes of Maturity." *Canadian Literature* 72 (1977): 69–74.
Attar, Farid ud-Din. *The Conference of the Birds.* Trans. Afkham Darbandi and Dick Davis. Middlesex: Penguin, 1984.
Bashiri, Iraj. *The Fiction of Sadeq Hedayat.* Lexington, Kentucky: Mazda, 1984.
Beard, Michael and Hasan Javady. "Iranian Writers Abroad: Survey and Elegy." *World Literature Today*, 60.2 (1986): 257–61.
Beeman, William O. *Language, Status, and Power in Iran.* Bloomington: Indiana University Press, 1986.
Bencheikh, Jamel Eddine. "Islam et Littérature." *Le Monde* 7 April 1989: 17.
"Books Reveal Tribulations of Turkish Women." *The German Tribune* 9 February 1986: 9.
Browne, Edward, G. *A Literary History of Persia.* Vol. II. Cambridge: University Press, 1956.
Brugman, J. *An Introduction to the History of Modern Arabic Literature in Egypt.* Leiden: E. J. Brill, 1984.
Cachia, Pierre. "Introduction to *An Egyptian Childhood.*" Trans. E. H. Paxton. Washington. D.C.: Three Continents, 1981.
——. *Tāhā Husayn: His Place in the Egyptian Literary Renaissance.* London: Luzac, 1956.
Carmichael, Lachlan. "Nobel Laureate Faces Threats for Novel 'Offensive' to Islam." *The Globe and Mail* 28 April 1989: A16.
Daniel, Norman. *Islam and the West: The Making of an Image.* Edinburgh: University Press, 1960.
Dasenbrock, Reed. "Intelligibility and Meaningfulness in Multicultural Literature in English." *PMLA* 102 (1987): 10–19.
Déjeux, Jean. *Assia Djebar: romancière algérienne cinéaste arabe.* Sherbrooke, Québec: Naaman, 1984.
Dubois, Lionel. "Interview de Driss Chraïbi." *Revue Celfan Review*, 5.2 (1986), 20–6.
Durix, Jean-Pierre. "The Artistic Journey in Salman Rushdie's *Shame.*" *World Literature Written in English* 23 (1984): 451–63.
Foucault, Michel. *L'Archéologie du savoir.* Paris: Gallimard, 1969.
Goldhammer, Kurt. *Der Mythus von Ost und West: Eine Kultur-und religionsgeschichtliche Betrachtung.* München: Ernst Reinhardt, 1962.
Grady, Wayne, "The Other Canadian." *Books in Canada* 11.5 (1982): 9–11.
Greenbaum, Jessica. "A Minority of One." *The Houstonian Magazine* June 1986: 51–3.
Haywood, John A. *Modern Arabic Literature 1800–1970: An Introduction with Extracts in Translation.* New York: St. Martin's, 1972.
Hegel, Georg Wilhelm Friedrich. *Lectures on the Philosophy of Religion.* Vol. III. Trans. R. F. Brown et al. Ed. Peter C. Hodgson. Berkeley: University of California Press, 1985.
Hillmann, Michael C. Ed. *Hedayat's* The Blind Owl: *Forty Years After.* Middle East Monographs, 4. Austin: University of Texas Press, 1978.

——. *A Lonely Woman: Forugh Farrokhzad and her Poetry*. Washington D.C.: Three Continents and Mage, 1987.
Hollington, Michael. "Salman Rushdie's *Shame*." *Meanjin* 43 (1984): 403–7.
"Interview with Salman Rushdie." *Contemporary Authors* 111 (1984): 414–17.
Javadi, Hasan. "Women in Persian Literature: An Explanatory Study." In *Women and the Family in Iran*, ed. A. Fathi. Leiden: E. J. Brill, 1985. 37–59.
Johansen, Ib. "The Flight from the Enchanter: Reflections on Salman Rushdie's *Grimus*." *Kunapipi* 7.1 (1985): 20–32.
Kamshad, Hassan. *Modern Persian Prose Literature*. Cambridge: University Press, 1966.
Lawrence, T. E. *Seven Pillars of Wisdom*. Seventh edition. London: Jonathan Cape, 1942.
Lazard, Gilbert. "Sadegh Hedayat, précurseur du nouveau reálisme iranien." *Le Figaro Littéraire* February 1954: 4.
Lejeune, Philippe. *Le Pacte autobiographique*. Paris: Seuil, 1975.
Lewis, Bernard. *The Muslim Discovery of Europe*. New York: W. W. Norton, 1982.
Louca, Anouar, *Voyageurs et écrivains égyptiens en France au XIXe Siècle*. Paris: Didier, 1970.
Mikhail, Mona. *Images of Arab Women: Fact and Fiction*. Washington D.C.: Three Continents, 1979.
Malti-Douglas, Fedwa. *Blindness and Autobiography: Al-Ayyām of Tāhā Husayn*. Princeton: University Press, 1988.
Modarressi, Taghi. "Salman Rushdie and the Immigrant's Dilemma." *The Washington Post* 12 March 1989: 7.
Moïn, Mohammad. *Farhang-e Moïn*. Vol. V. Tehran: Amir Kabir, 1967.
Moosa, Matti. *The Origins of Modern Arabic Fiction*. Washington, D.C.: Three Continents, 1983.
Morier, James. *The Adventures of Hajji Baba of Isphahan*. Rpt; New York: Random House, 1937.
Mottahedeh, Roy. *The Mantle of the Prophet: Religion and Politics in Iran*. New York: Simon and Schuster, 1985.
Nicholson, Reynold A. Ed. and trans. *Selected Poems from the Divani Shamsi Tabriz*. Rpt. Cambridge: University Press, 1977.
"Notes and Remarks." *Kayhan-e Farhangi* 3 (November 1986): 43–4.
"Our Only Arab-Jewish-French-Canadian Author." *Saturday Night* 1 (1979): 9.
Owen, I. M. "Bridge of Tongues. Why an Arab-speaking, Baghdad-born Jew is a Perfect Guide to the Modern Canadian Experience." *Books in Canada* 12 (1976): 5–6.
Parameswaran, Uma. "Handcuffed to History: Salman Rushdie's Art." *Ariel* 14 (1983): 34–45.
Raffat, Donné. *The Prison Papers of Bozorg Alavi: A Literary Odyssey*. Syracuse: Syracuse University Press, 1985.
Ricks, Thomas M. *Critical Perspectives on Modern Persian Literature*. Washington D.C.: Three Continents, 1984.
Robb, Christina. "Review of *The Book of Absent People*." *The Boston Globe* 7 March 1986: 12.
Rushdie, Salman. "Interview and Commentary: *Midnight's Children* and *Shame*." *Kunapipi* 7.1 (1985): 1–19.
Sajjadieh, Seyyed Mohammad Ali. "How the Nobel Prize is Granted." *Kayhan-e Farhangi* 3 (December 1986): 36.
Schwab, Raymond. *La Renaissance orientale*. Paris: Payot, 1950.

Semah, David. *Four Egyptian Literary Critics.* Leiden: E. J. Brill, 1974.
Shaheen, Mohammad. "Tayeb Salih and Conrad." *Comparative Literature Studies* 22 (1985): 156–71.
Simard, Sylvain. "Naïm Kattan: La Promesse du temps retrouvé." *Voix et Images* 11 (1985): 33–44.
Tournier, Michel. "Préface à *Adieu Babylone.*" Paris: Julliard, 1976.
Visram, Rozina. *Ayahs, Lascars and Princes: Indians in Britain 1700–1947.* London: Pluto, 1986.
Wright, Denis. *The Persians Amongst the English: Episodes in Anglo-Persian History.* London: I. B. Tauris, 1985.

Index

Abed-Rabbo, Samir, 107
Abu-Khalil, Asad, 100, 107
Abu-Lughod, Ibrahim, 16–17, 20
Ahmad Sinân Celebi, 3
Ajami, Fouad, 106
Alavi, Bozorg, 64, 65
Al-e Ahmad, Jalal, 97, 102–104, 106, 108
Allard, Jacques, 28, 30, 75
Allen, Roger, 69
Alloula, Malek, 39–41, 42, 70
Amir-Shahy, Mahshid, 73, 83
Attar, Farid ud-Din, 79, 83, 84, 85, 86, 88
Avery Peter, 21
al-Azhar, 24, 25, 27, 28, 113
Beeman, William O., 21
Berber, 34, 35
Bildungsroman, 30
Boullata, Kamal, 41
Browne, Edward G., 89, 117
Brugman, J., 26
al-Bustāni, Brutus, 18
Cachia, Pierre, 26, 27
Chraïbi, Driss, 33–36, 55
Cragg, Kenneth, 24, 107
Daniel, Norman, 2, 15
Dasenbrock, R., 82–83
Delacroix, Eugène, 38
Derrida, Jacques, 7
Djebar, Assia, 53–54
Eurocentrism, iii, 11, 88, 108
Fanon, Frantz, 104, 109
Farukhzad, Furugh, 42–44
Flaubert, Gustave, 37
Foucault, Michel, 2, 6, 8, 9, 23
Frankification (*tafarnuj*), 18
Franks, 2
Freud, 105
Freudian interpretation, 67, 69
Goethe, J. W. von, 8

Goldhammer, Kurt, 2
Greenbaum, Jessica, 96
Hedayat, Sadegh, 64, 71, 99, 111, 114, 117; *The Blind Owl*, 65–67, 91; "The Caravan of Islam," 88–92
Hegel, G. W. F., 1, 113
Hikmet, Nizam, 37
Hillmann, Michael C., 42, 67
Hollington, Michael, 59
Husain, Tāhā, 28, 33, 55, 114, 117; *Al-Ayyām* (*A Passage to France*), 23–27; *Adīb*, 27; *Fī al-Adab al-Jāhilī*, 26; *Future of Culture in Egypt*, 26
Hussain, Asaf, 6, 107
Ibn Batoutah, 2
Iqbal, Mohammad, 4–5, 12
Iranian revolution, 8, 103, 105, 111, 112, 115
Ishāq, Adīb, 18
Kabbani, Rana, 3, 6, 37–39, 41, 111
Kamal, Ihsan, 41–42
Kamshad, Hassan, 22, 65
Kattan, Naïm, 29, 75, 117; *Adieu Babylone*, 27–28, 30–33, 75; *La Fiancée promise*, 31; *Les Fruits arrachés*, 31, 32; "Le Gardien de l'alphabet," 73–74
Kayhan-e Farhangi, 112–113
Khatibi, Abdelkebir, 6, 117; *Maghreb pluriel*, 76, 109–110; *La Mémoire tatouée*, 72, 75
Khayyam, Omar, 64–65
Khomeini, Ruhollah (Ayatollah), 100, 101–102
Lawrence, T. E., 8, 117
Lazard, Gilbert, 64
Lejeune, Philippe, 30, 62
Lewis, Bernard, 13, 107
Louca, Anouar, 18, 20
al-Ma'ari, 25

INDEX

Mahfouz, Naguib, 113
Malti-Douglas, Fedwa, 23, 24, 25
Massignon, Louis, 8
Modarressi, Taghi, 79–83, 88, 116, 117
Moïn, Mohammad, 85
Morier, James (*The Adventures of Hajji Baba of Isphahan*), 21–22, 58
Mottahedeh, Roy, 80, 100, 101, 104, 105
Mukherjee, Bharati, 72, 77, 88; *Days and Nights in Calcutta*, 55–59; *Wife*, 48–51, 53, 54
Nasir-i-Khusraw, 89
Nasir ud-Din Shah, 4, 15–16
Nerval, Gérard de, 8
Nesin, Aziz, 97–99, 117
Nu'ayma, Mikha'il, 20
Nyang, Sulayman S., 107
Occidentalism, 2, 6, 11, 116, 117
Orientalism, iii, 6, 7, 9, 103, 107, 110, 111, 116, 117
Ottoman Empire, 16
Ottoman historians, 3
Parthasarathy, R., 77
Pezeshkzad, Iraj, 92–94, 99
Qulzum, 111
Qureshi, Jamil, 107
Rachlin, Nahid, 108–109
Reza Shah, 65
Rushdie, Salman, 111; *Grimus*, 61–62, 83–88, 114; (*Midnight's Children*, 62, 63; *The Satanic Verses*, 26, 113–117; *Shame*, 59–64, 115, 116
al-Saadawy, Nawal, 47, 54

Sadiq, Isa, 19
al-Sadr, Musa (Imam), 106
Said, Edward W., 6, 36, 38, 111, 116; *After the Last Sky*, 5, 7, 56, 73; *Covering Islam*, 10–11, 100–111; *Orientalism*, 2, 3, 5, 7–10, 37
Said, Laila, 45–47
Saleh, Sanniya, 41, 42, 44
Salih, Tayeb, 67–71, 72
Scheinhardt, Saliha, 37, 76; *Frauen die sterben ohne daß sie gelebt hätten*, 51–54
Schwab, Raymond, 2
Semah, David, 26
Shah Abbas, 13
Shaheen, Mohammad, 69, 71
Shamsi Tabriz, 55
Shariati, Ali, 102, 104–106, 108
al-Shaykh, Hanan, 44–45
Sherley, Anthony (Sir), 13
Shi'ism, 14, 103, 104, 105
Shirazi, Manny, 77, 79
Sidhwa, Bapsi, 94–96, 99
Simard, Sylvain, 33
Steinem, Gloria, 46–47
Soyinka, Wole, 112–113
at-Tahtāwi, Rifa'a, 17–18
Tournier, Michel, 28
Tugay, Emine Foat, 16
Uruch Beg (*Don Juan of Persia*), 13–16, 18, 89, 92
Visram, Rozina, 19
Wright, Denis, 19, 92